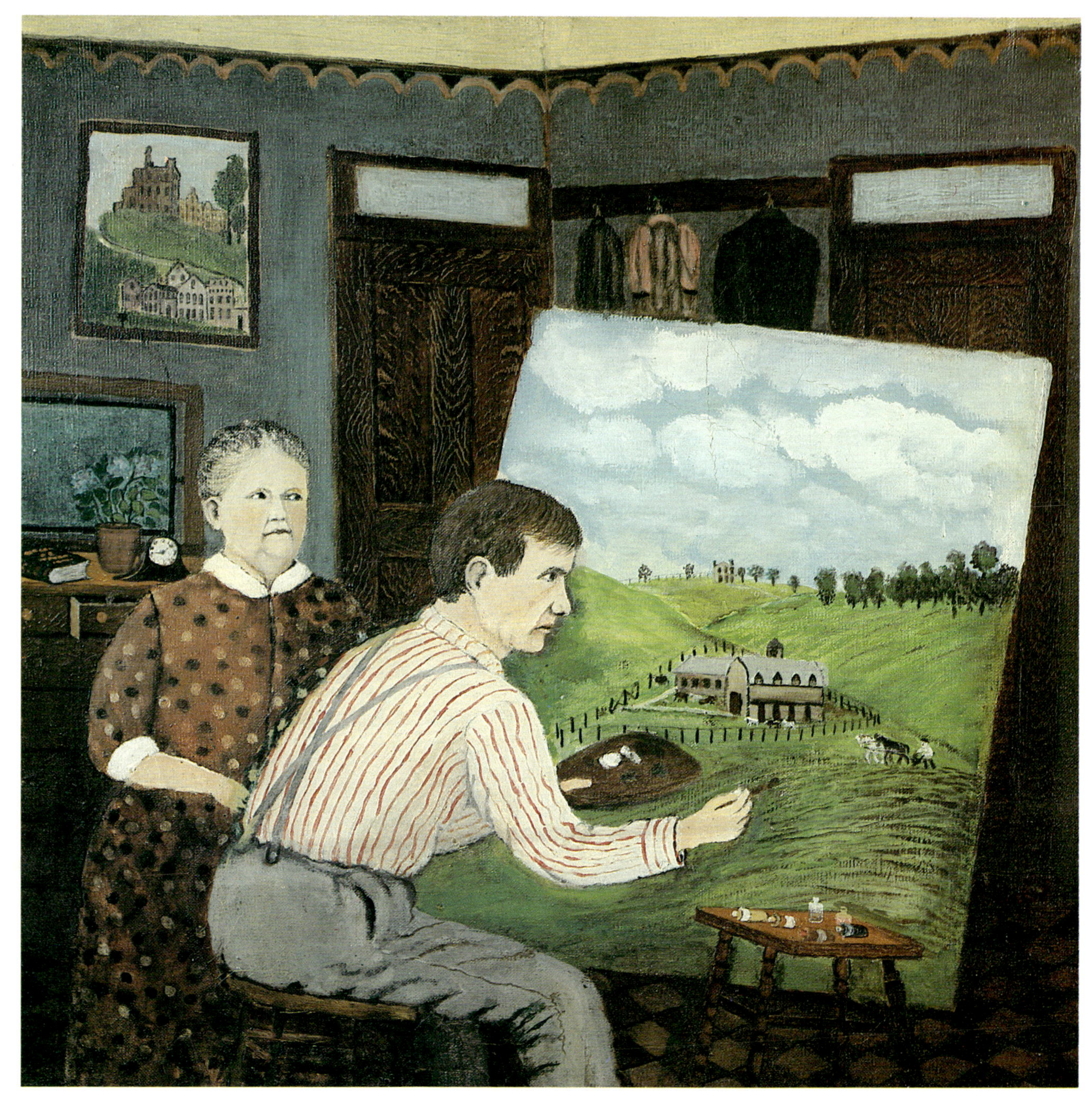

JOHN KANE
MODERN AMERICA'S FIRST FOLK PAINTER

With an Essay by Jane Kallir

GALERIE ST. ETIENNE, NEW YORK

John Kane: Modern America's First Folk Painter

Exhibition dates:
April 17–May 25, 1984
Galerie St. Etienne, New York, New York

February 2–March 31, 1985
Museum of Art, Carnegie Institute, Pittsburgh, Pennsylvania

Cover: Detail from **John Kane and His Wife**.
Frontispiece: **John Kane and His Wife**. Circa 1928. 23″ x 23″.

Designed by Gary Cosimini
Printed by Rapoport Printing Corp., New York
ISBN: 0-910810-24-9

<u>Foreword</u>

Among the great artists of this century, John Kane holds a unique position. Discovered at a time when folk art was still intimately linked with the development of modern art, he was the first American folk artist to win fame in his own lifetime, and the last to have his works placed alongside those of the most progressive American painters. Kane initially won recognition at the age of sixty-seven when one of his paintings — a work both naive and powerfully sincere — was accepted in Pittsburgh's Carnegie International Exhibition. National acclaim came quickly. Kane's paintings were sought after by such celebrities as Clare Booth Luce, Cecil Beaton and Clifford Odets, and today hang in many of the nation's major museums. The Carnegie Institute played an active role in encouraging the artist's career, and it is fitting that the Carnegie has come to house the largest single collection of his work.

Today, exactly fifty years after Kane's death, it is appropriate to pay tribute to his achievement. One of the most fascinating aspects of the current exhibition is its inclusion of the artist's working drawings, none of which has been previously either reproduced or exhibited. We should be grateful to the Galerie St. Etienne, which has spared no effort to assemble this retrospective and produce this catalogue.

Henry Adams, Curator of Fine Arts
Museum of Art, Carnegie Institute, Pittsburgh

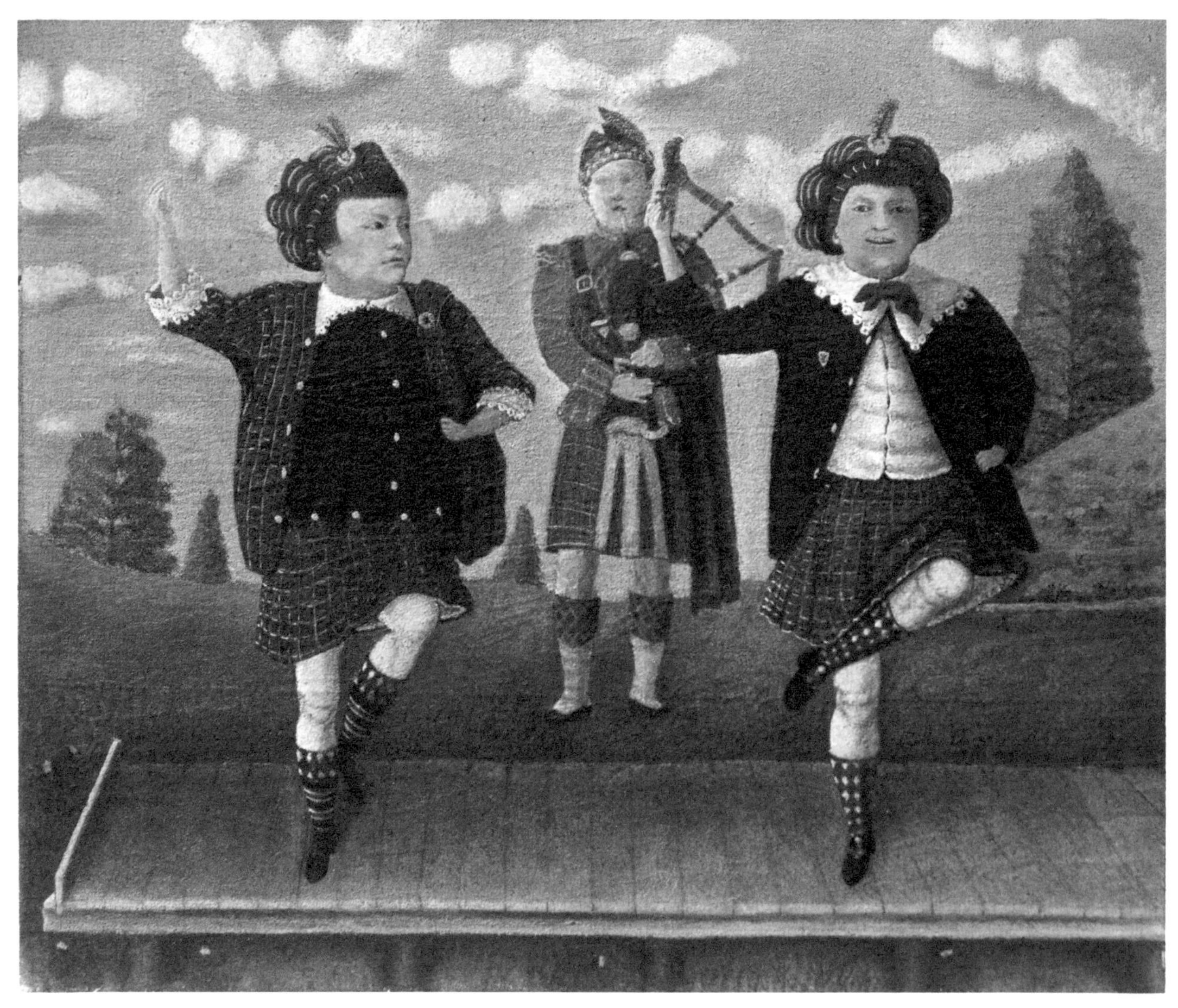

1. **Scene in the Scottish Highlands**. Circa 1927. 22¾″ x 27″. Museum of Art, Carnegie Institute; Gift of G. David Thompson, 1959.

In the autumn of 1927, John Kane lived in a desolate area of Pittsburgh known locally as the "Strip." Across the Allegheny River from the Heinz pickle factory, and next to the Pennsylvania Railroad tracks, he eked out a meager existence in a one-room flat. The trains that rushed by his second-floor window on elevated tracks drowned out any attempt at conversation, but it was a problem Kane seldom noticed, for he had few visitors. Paintings were stacked two and three deep along the shabby walls of his apartment, forcing his iron bedstead (virtually the only piece of furniture, save a single chair and a stove) into the center of the room. The floor was covered with crumpled pieces of paper, laid down to catch stray splatters of paint. In the vestibule outside hung a brown card bearing the legend, "John Kane, House Painter."

Throughout the remainder of 1927 and in the early months of 1928, a number of reporters would make the treck to Kane's humble quarters, read the tattered sign, and smile. For John Kane, house painter, had accomplished the impossible: he had, on his third try, "crashed" the Carnegie Institute's prestigious Annual International Exhibition of Paintings. The sixty-seven-year-old Scotsman with his wooden leg and worn overalls might look like a common laborer, but men of uncommon judgement had declared him an artist. It was an unprecedented turn of events, and one that took many people a good deal of time to accept.

The notion of the talented amateur was not entirely new to art circles. Prior to World War I, Europe's pioneer modernists, seeking to escape from the stranglehold of the academic system, sought inspiration in the work of those who had never received formal training in art. Henri Rousseau, the painting toll-collector whose jungle fantasies captivated Pablo Picasso and his comrades, demonstrated the authentic power of the "naive" vision. Regarded as a joke even by his artist friends, Rousseau rose to fame alongside them when, after the war, the avant-garde suddenly began to be taken seriously. America's growing awareness of the European art scene brought the legend of Rousseau to the New World, where it came to rest, finally, with the jury of the Carnegie International. Andrew Dasburg, a painter who had himself tried to emulate the self-taught artist's spontaneity, convinced the jury to accept Kane's entry, *Scene in the Scottish Highlands* (Plate 1), by purchasing the picture for his own collection.[1]

From the moment his participation in the Carnegie International was made public, Kane became the unwilling plaything of the press. Most of the reporters who made the pilgrimage to the "Strip" saw Kane as the proverbial talking dog: remarkable not because he painted well, but because he was painting at all. They could no more understand the Carnegie's selection criteria than could their average reader; what they wanted was a human-interest story. With their inherent flair for tragedy, the Pittsburgh tabloids turned the artist's latter-day career into a procession of little scandals. Kane's enduring poverty, the bitterest irony of his so-called success, became the subject of numerous vulgar headlines. "Facing Eviction, Strip Painter Gets Glory But No Cash," was the lead-in to a story describing his decision to move to new quarters following an unwarranted rent increase.[2] At one point, it was gleefully (and erroneously) announced that the starving artist was compelled to return to house painting in order to make ends meet. Kane's death from tuberculosis in 1934 was transformed into a garish media event, with photographers recording the final agonies of the emaciated, semi-conscious man, while reporters daily debated his financial health in print.

Of all the petty controversies surrounding Kane during his seven years in the limelight, the worst was a deliberate exposé staged simultaneously by two leading newspapers, *The Pittsburgh Press* and the *Sun Telegraph*. From the start, the press was inclined to view the Carnegie's acceptance of Kane as a hoax, and local painters resented the fact (stressed repeatedly in the attendant publicity) that he was the only Pittsburgh artist to be so honored.[3] One such jealous colleague, Milan Petrovits, decided that Kane's pictures were painted over photographs. On the occasion of Kane's first one-man show, mounted by the Pittsburgh Junior League in 1931, Petrovits convinced the *Sun Telegraph* to purchase one of the suspect paintings, and proved his point with varnish remover. The competing journal, not to be outdone, purchased another painting and did likewise. That evening, both papers published the evidence that everyone had been clamoring for: John Kane was a fraud.

For days the issue was bandied about in the press. Kane explained that the photo-paintings had been done long ago and that all his prize-winning canvases were purely freehand. Eventually X-rays bore him out. Artists and museum officials rallied to his defense. Samuel Harden Church, president of the Carnegie Institute, declared that the scandal would in no way alter the artist's standing with the museum. In fact, Kane had already been invited to participate in that year's International, an honor that meant he could bypass the jury and choose his own entry.

By the time of the photography exposé, it was clear that Kane's inclusion in the 1927 Carnegie International had been no fluke. In 1928 the jury had accepted his painting *Old Clinton Furnace* (Plate 28), and after he again won admission the following year, the headlines finally declared, "Kane, House Painter, Ceases to be Joke."[4] The impact of the Carnegie showings was bolstered by other exhibitions. In 1928, '29, and '33 the "house painter" took prizes at the Annual Exhibition of the Associated Artists of Pittsburgh. In 1929, he was invited to participate in a group show at Harvard. In 1930, his Carnegie International entry, *Across the Strip* (Plate 19), was purchased by the Phillips Collection in Washington, D.C., the first museum to own a Kane. As the artist began to be better known outside Pittsburgh, he acquired such well-heeled patrons as Mrs. John D. Rockefeller and Professor John Dewey. In the first decade of its existence, New York's Museum of Modern Art placed Kane in no fewer than four surveys of contemporary trends, among them its fifth anniversary exhibition, "Modern Works of Art." He appeared in "annuals" at major museums such as the Art Institute of Chicago and the Cincinnati Art Museum, was included in the first and second Biennial Exhibitions of the Whitney Museum, and, until his death, continued to show every year at the Carnegie International.

During the 1930's, Kane's work was routinely exhibited alongside that of his more sophisticated colleagues, for "naive" or "folk" art was seen as a concomitant of the modern movement. Gradually, however, people became aware of folk art as a distinct category in its own right. Exhibitions such as the Museum of Modern Art's 1938 survey, "Masters of Popular Painting" (which naturally included Kane), encouraged this tendency, and as more self-taught artists were discovered, commercial galleries began consciously to develop a market for their work.[5] By the mid-1940s, New York had weathered its first folk art fad. From this time forward, folk art (representational, easily understood) and modern art (increasingly abstract and complicated) went their separate ways. Kane, however, remained tied to the earlier conception of the naive, as put forth by Picasso and the artist/theorist Wassily Kandinsky. He was "the American Rousseau," whose work, even today, is not segregated in our few specialized folk art museums, but rather may be found in the great public collections of twentieth-century art.

John Kane was the first American folk painter to win acclaim during his lifetime. The itinerant portraitists (or "limners"), who may be considered his nineteenth-century predecessors, had catered to a decidedly provincial clientele. Because their work, at the time, was of no interest to the cultural elite, it was documented in a fairly haphazard way. One of the benefits of Kane's fame, on the other hand, was that it led to the preservation of biographical data that would otherwise have been lost. Much of the credit for this belongs to Marie McSwigan, a newspaper reporter who transcribed the artist's autobiography and published it under the title *Sky Hooks*.

According to *Sky Hooks*, John Kane first saw the light of day on August 19, 1860, in West Calder, Scotland. His parents had emigrated from Ireland in hopes of improving their lot, but found circumstances not much better in Scotland. At his own insistence, John went to work in the shale mines at the age of nine. The following year, Mr. Cain (as the name was then spelled)[6] died, leaving his widow and seven children to fend for themselves. John, who had completed only the third grade, was never able to return to school full time, though he occasionally attended night classes when he did not have to work. Mrs. Cain eventually remarried, and the family began to prosper modestly. However, John's stepfather nurtured a belief that they could do even better in America and went to seek his fortune there. In 1879 John joined his stepfather in Pennsylvania, and before long they had saved enough money to bring the rest of the family across the Atlantic.

During the next years, Kane roamed about the Pittsburgh area, from McKeesport to Connellsville to Braddock, and then went south to Alabama, Tennessee and Kentucky in search of work. Buffeted from one job to the next by the vicissitudes of the economy, he helped build the Baltimore and Ohio Railroad, worked in a tubing factory, a coal mine, a steel mill, and as a construction worker and street paver. "I was always on the lookout for better jobs," he wrote. "The wages interested me the most. The amount of work, the hardness of it, the hours and all like that, didn't worry me a bit." He was a powerful man, able to handle the most gruelling factory work and even to hold his own in the boxing ring.

Kane had returned to Braddock and was living near his family, when his career as a "brawnyman" came to an end. Cutting across the Baltimore and Ohio Railroad yards late one night, he and his companions were surprised by an unlit train. John pushed his cousin to safety, only to get his own leg caught on the track. Thirty-one at the time, he became a one-legged laborer with limited employment opportunities. It took him some months to recover from his accident, but he was not one to be permanently discouraged by misfortune. Balancing gracefully on his wooden prosthesis became one more skill to be mastered, and only in the last years of his life did a noticeable limp betray his handicap. Nevertheless, with his physical prowess diminished, Kane had a more difficult time finding work, and when he did finally land a job as a railroad watchman, it was at substantially reduced wages. He needed to develop abilities better suited to his new limitations, and it was thus that he got involved, bit by bit, with painting.

In 1897, John Kane married Maggie Halloran, and the following year their first child, Mary, was born. Family obligations made it imperative for Kane to seek a higher paying job, and so he went to work painting railroad cars for the Pressed Steel Car Company in McKees Rocks. Here he found a passion that would outlast everything else in his tenuous, tragedy-prone life. "I . . . became in love with paint," he said quite simply. At noon, while the other men were eating, Kane would slip back into the rail yards and cover the sides of the bare boxcars with pictures. Much to his relief, the foreman did not object, so long as the artist's concoctions were painted over after the lunch break. From this first encounter with paint, Kane learned methods and techniques that he never abandoned. With just the three primary colors, lightened or darkened with white or black, he was able to duplicate every shade under the sun. He developed a permanent disdain for pre–mixed colors and later insisted that "the best thing in the world for a young artist would be to hire himself out to a good painting contractor."

When the boxcar business slackened and Kane was laid off, he decided to put his new knowledge of paint to practical use. Like the limners of yore, he went door-to-door offering to paint people's likenesses. The invention of the camera had essentially put the limners out of business, but to Kane photography was a boon. He found that his customers generally had snapshots, often of a departed relative, that they wanted enlarged and embellished. He made the enlargements himself, or had them done commercially, and then colored them in paint or pastel.[7] This was the origin of the photo-paintings that, so many years later, would cause the artist such grief.

Few of Kane's photo-paintings (and none from this early period) survive. Judging from the available examples done later in his career, his commissioned portraits well exceeded the limits of conventional retouching. Whereas the retoucher normally works in glazes, preserving the underlying structure of the photograph, Kane obliterated the image entirely. Often he would allow an element of fantasy to impinge upon his photographic base. *Margie and Friend, Eleanor Clancy* (Plate 2), the earliest extant painting that can be dated, is actually a composite of photographic and freehand images, for the flowering field is pure invention. Ironically, *Dad's Payday* (Plate 3), one of the two paintings unmasked by the Pittsburgh newspapers, supports more than it damns Kane's artistic talents. Comparison of the exposed and painted halves permits a before-and-after examination of the transformation the artist effected on a rather banal snapshot. His sensitivity to the photograph's intrinsic formal qualities caused him to isolate and exaggerate block shapes, creating a more stylized and aesthetically pleasing composition. More important, however, is the emotional quality with which he invested the children, who reminded him of his own. The resultant painting depicts not actual people, but the feeling in his heart. The photograph so moved him that he also made a freehand enlargement, *Expectations* (Plate 4), with an expanded background that better matched his interpretation of the subject. Today, when the incorporation of photo-derived imagery—whether through collage, photo-silkscreen, or the meticulous blow-ups created by the photorealists—has become routine practice, the question of Kane's originality hardly seems worth debating. However, it is interesting to note that Kane, in his nonchalant acceptance of the photograph as a natural adjunct to the fine arts, anticipated his more sophisticated successors by nearly half a century.

John Kane did well selling his photo-paintings—better, he claimed, than he did later with his larger, entirely original canvases. His little family flourished. A second daughter, Margaret, was born in 1901, but John dreamed of a son. In 1904 he got his wish, only to have it snuffed out when, a day after his

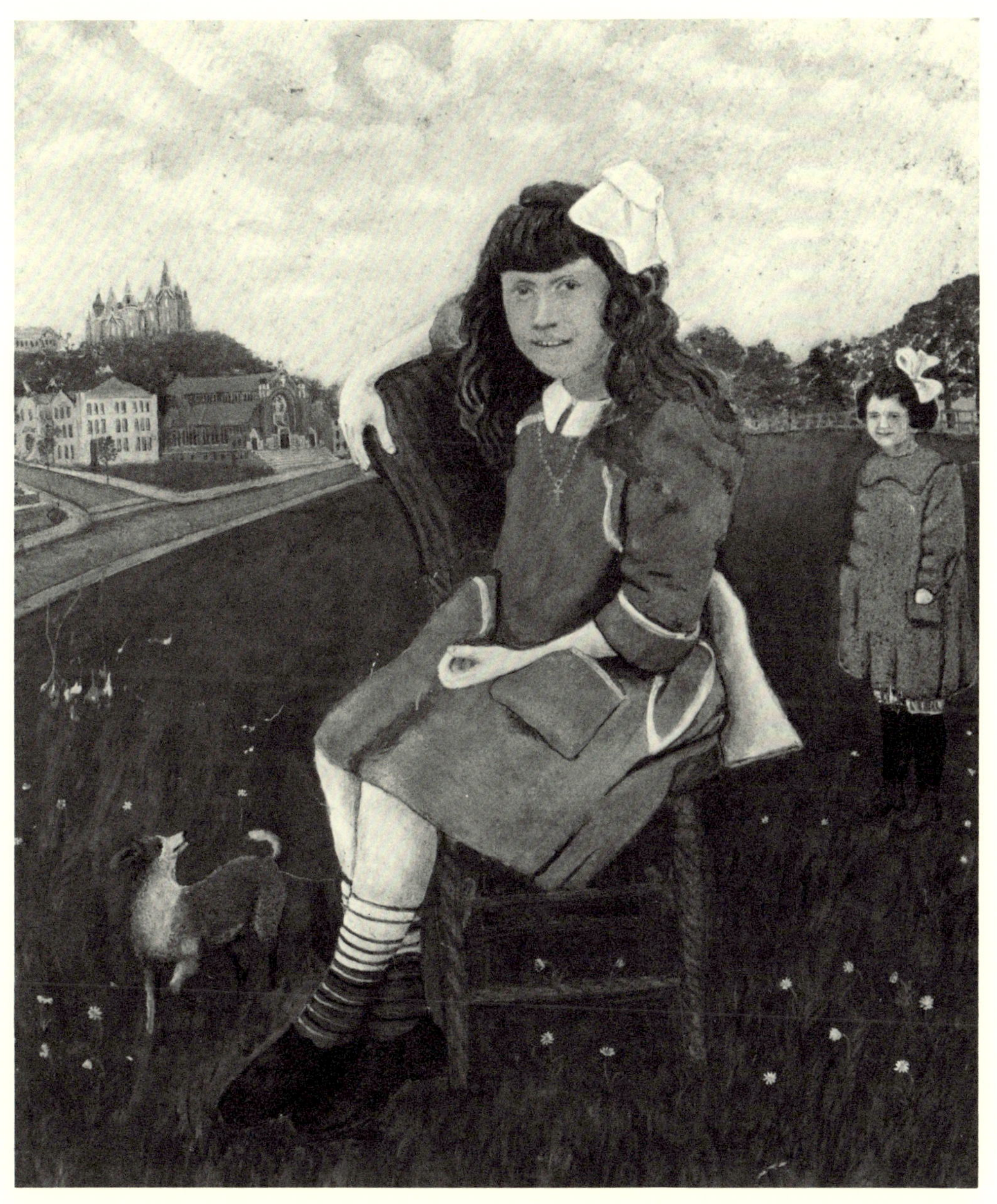

2. **Margie and Friend, Eleanor Clancy**. Circa 1915. Board. 21″ x 17″.

birth, the infant succumbed to typhoid fever. Kane had survived economic slumps and physical injury, but this was a blow from which he never fully recovered. He took to drink and temporarily lost all incentive to work. He left his family for long periods, finally losing track of them altogether. Only in 1927, when she read about the Carnegie International in a New York newspaper, did Mrs. Kane rejoin her husband. In the intervening years, the artist wandered about Pennsylvania, Ohio and West Virginia, eventually settling permanently in Pittsburgh. During periods of economic depression, he depended on the support of charitable organizations such as the Salvation Army. In better times, he found work as a house painter and carpenter.

Throughout these long, dreary years, Kane continually tried to find a place for art in his life. Once he attempted to apprentice himself to a muralist, who, though polite in his rejection, was undoubtedly scornful of the fledgling artist's qualifications. On several occasions, Kane considered enrolling in art school, but in each instance the tuition was too high. So he worked on his own. Scraps of beaver board picked up on one of his construction jobs gave him the material on which to create some of his first independent compositions. Recalling his success with the photo-paintings, he executed unsolicited freehand "portraits" of local houses, and then endeavored to sell them to the residents. As he had done all his life, he learned "on the job," through trial and error, the secrets of his chosen craft. Humbly acknowledging that academically trained artists had an advantage over him, he nonetheless felt proud of his self-made accomplishments. "Often in the past I have been at a loss to know how to overcome some significant point in artistic form that I would have learned easily in an art school," he said. "But my spirit of observation has helped me to acquire knowledge and so the source of my information did not matter."

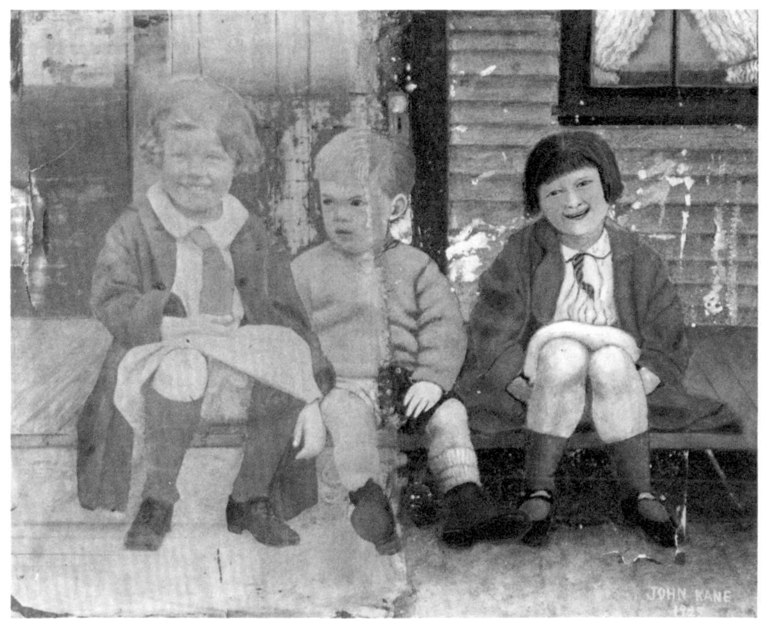

3. **Dad's Payday.**
1925. Board.
16″ x 20″.

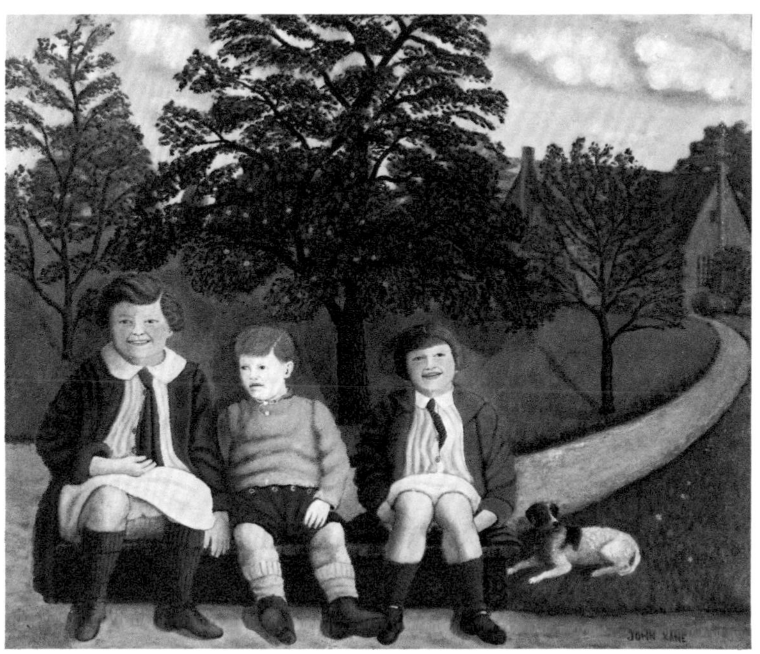

4. **Expectations.**
Circa 1925-26.
Board. 23″ x 27″.

In order to teach himself, John Kane haunted the only halls of knowledge that were open to him: the public museums and libraries. From these sources he developed a hazy awareness of the procedures and subjects of the "fine" artist. A paucity of models must have hampered his efforts to draw from life, but he apparently got around this problem by sketching stationary figures on park benches, streetcars, or in railroad stations (Plates 6 and 7). According to his daughter, Margaret Corbett, Kane spent hours in the library copying pictures from illustrated art books. A lengthy series of facial studies, which bear no discernable relationship to his paintings, was probably done simply as a learning exercise. Some of these (Plate 5) were obviously inspired by an English-language edition of Charles le Brun's *Traité des passions*. The religious copies with which Kane initially tried to conquer the Carnegie International in 1925 and 1926 (Plate 8) undoubtedly reflect his conception of "serious" art. Such set pieces had been standard fare at the European salons of the preceding century, but Kane's copies did not qualify in Pittsburgh. On both occasions, his submissions were rejected: only original compositions, he was told, were allowed.

The indisputable fact that almost all folk painters have learned from copying was, for decades, a secret guarded closely by the sophisticates who championed their work. The myth of the naive, as put forth in the writings of Kandinsky, held that the untrained artist was a wellspring of creative innocence, whose primordial instincts remained untainted by the effects of an academic education. Thus it followed, or seemed to follow, that the nonacademic artist must be totally uninfluenced. For this reason, one of the Kane estate's earliest dealers advised the artist's heirs to burn all his smaller paintings and drawings.[8]

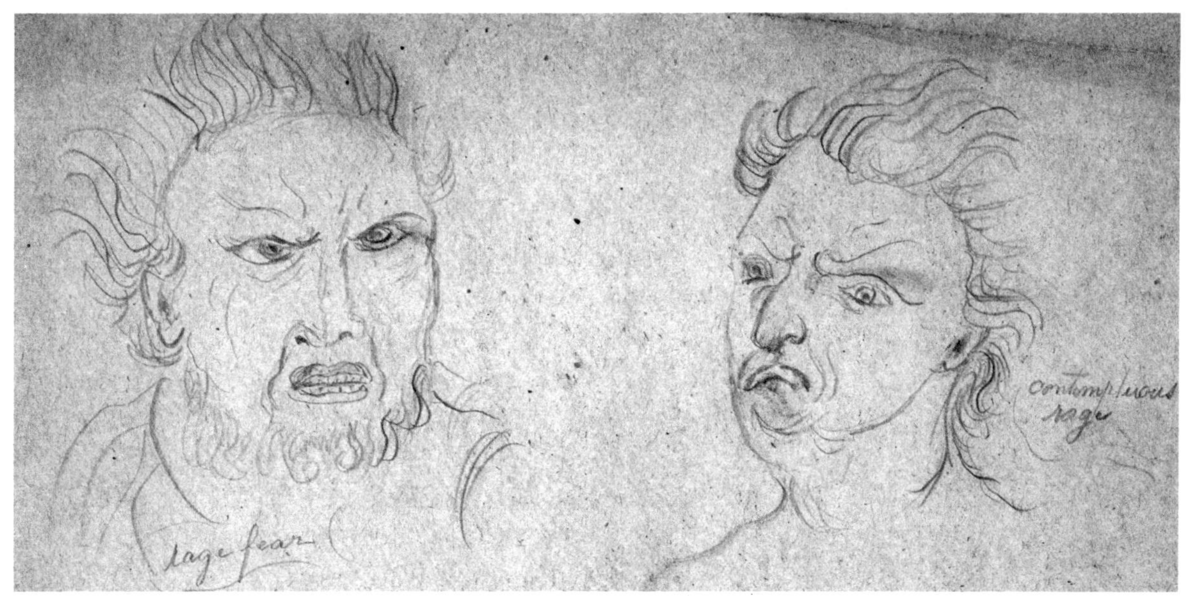

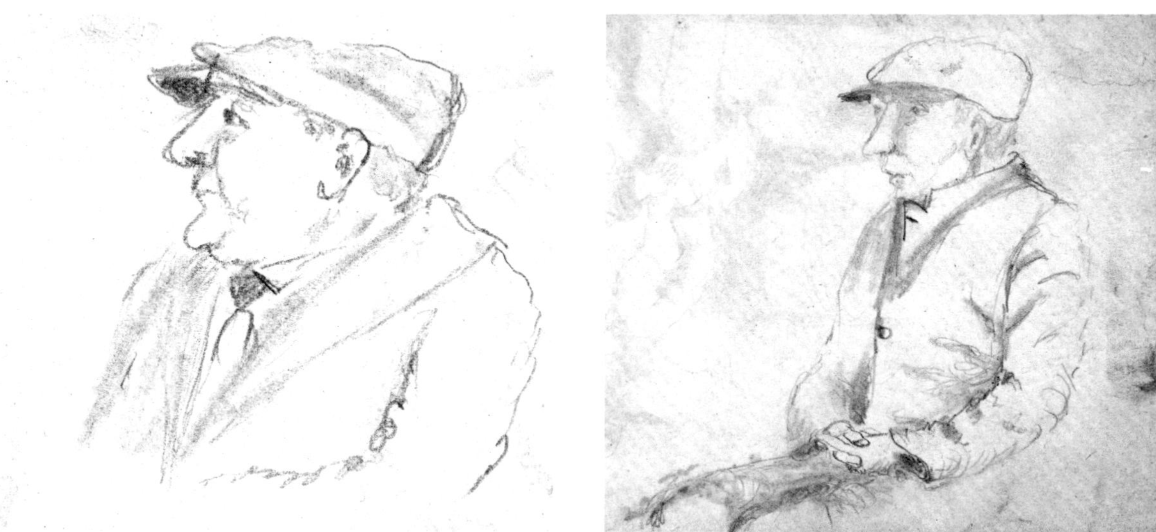

5. **Rage/Fear** and **Contemptuous Rage**. Pencil on paper. 7½″ x 10⅛″.
6. **Study of a Man**. Pencil on paper. 5½″ x 9″.
7. **Seated Man in Cap and Trenchcoat**. Pencil on paper. 5½″ x 9″.

Fortunately these instructions were not heeded, although this material was long kept hidden.

Kane, like any artist, was extraordinarily sensitive to the pictorial stimuli provided by his environment, for it is preposterous to suggest that art can develop in a complete visual vacuum. Folk artists, unlike their academic colleagues, never learn to subordinate themselves to a single tradition, but rather pick and choose from various traditions those elements best suited to their particular expressive needs. Kane was one of the first to understand that reliance on photographic or printed source images does not make an artist any less original, and his defense of such practices is worth quoting.

"All artists," Kane wrote, "are copying nature. They see the hills, the valleys, the trees and they copy those. If an artist sees something in a book he likes he will copy that, too, enlarging upon it or lessening it according to his requirements. So it makes no difference where he sees it, whether it is the work of nature or of another man or work in a book. He is bound to react to the inspiration he feels. He will copy in part and adapt and take out what he likes."

Kane's explanation of copying is also as good a description as has been written of the way in which he evolved the original landscape compositions that are considered his most important work. He outlined his methods as follows: "First of all, I have to see something which commands itself to my attention for one quality only, namely beauty. I first notice it, then I observe it well. Then I go back and visit it as often as necessary, noting the things I want to include in my painting." The 85 landscape drawings that survive[9] make it clear that Kane assembled his paintings piecemeal from a multitude of isolated images (Plates 24, 25 and 26). The procedure was not particularly systematic or

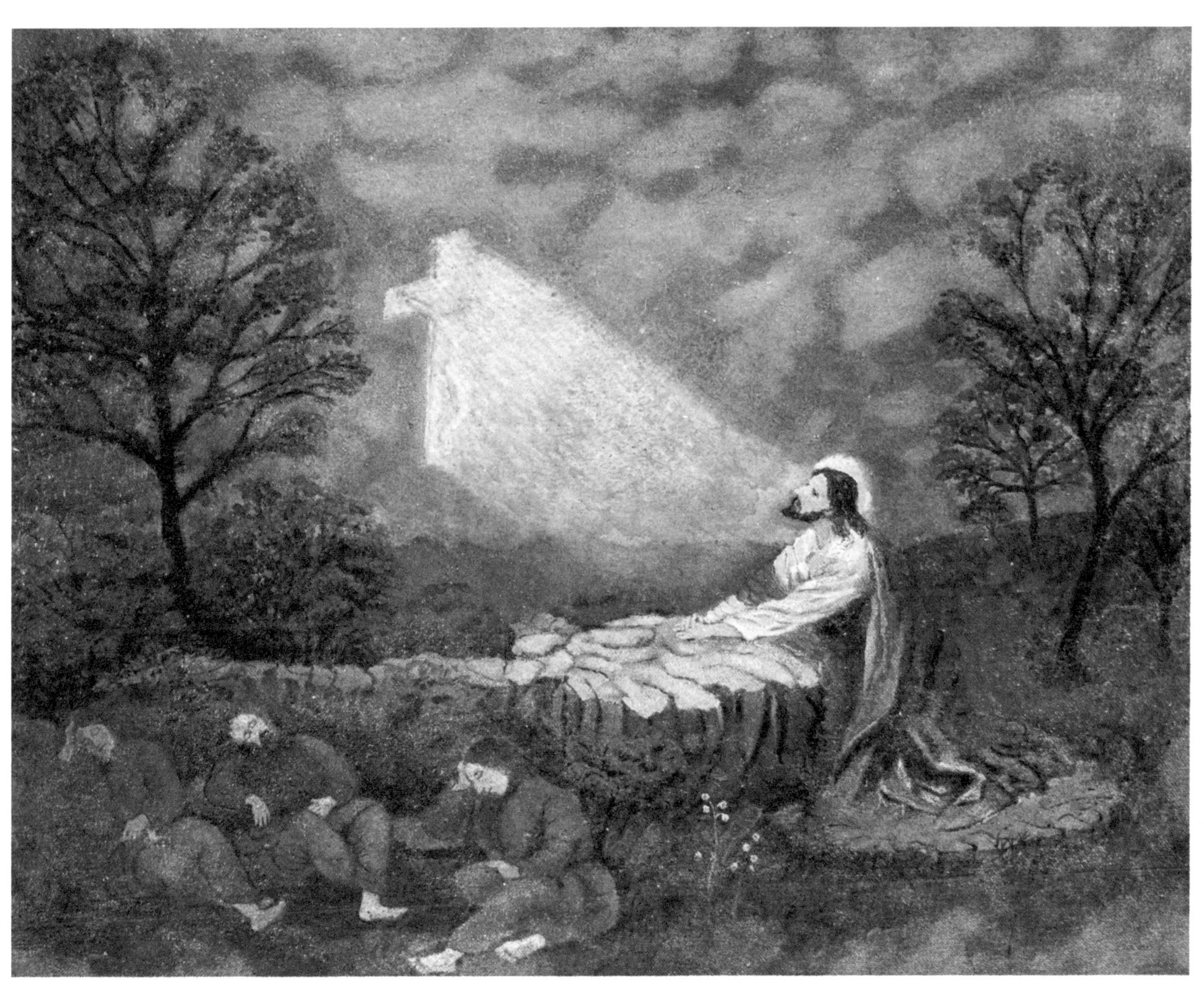

8. **The Agony in the Garden (Small Version).** 1926 or earlier. 16¼″ x 19¾″.

logical: it is unlikely that everything in his paintings was sketched out in advance, and sometimes several vignettes that would eventually appear on entirely different canvases were drawn on the same sheet of paper. Not a single drawing depicts a complete composition. In the final painting, elements were often freely transposed or eliminated entirely. The result was less a reflection of an actual scene than of the artist's mental image of that scene.

There is little doubt that all Kane's landscape drawings were done from nature. By his own account, he had been making such studies since the 1880s with no change in method or manner. Starting around 1910, he routinely carried his painting supplies with him so that he could make on-the-spot color sketches whenever the mood hit him. Although his finished paintings were generally executed in his apartment studio, he thought it imperative to get the color right by matching it on location, and was dismayed when a change in weather or time of day threw the tonal balance off. He claimed that he often worked up full-fledged oil studies in this manner, but it is not clear whether any of the duplicate scenes that recur in his oeuvre (Plates 22 and 23) were intended as "trial paintings."

Given Kane's habit of careful observation, it is unlikely that the "errors" or omissions in his landscape paintings were entirely accidental. In order to incorporate everything he considered important in a single canvas, he had to leave some things out. He had a tendency to tighten up or compress "empty" spaces. Alternatively, he might make a tree-covered hillside more interesting by filling it with little houses. In some instances, this was an act of pure imagination, and in others he merely "removed" concealing foliage to reveal buildings that were actually there. Comparison of the two versions (one of them unfinished) of *Juniata River* (Plates 17 and 18) with a photograph (Plate 16) from which Kane apparently worked reveals some of his typical alterations. Houses that can barely be identified in the photograph are brought into the open, and vaguely silhouetted hills are cut sharply against the sky.

Although it was reported that Kane carried a small box camera to aid in his study of the landscape,[10] it was also true, as he boasted at the time of the photo-painting scandal, that "no camera was ever constructed to get the view of objects that I, as an artist, see and paint." Once Kane had established the boundaries of the vista he wanted to depict, he became curious about details that could not necessarily be seen from the vantage point he had chosen.[11] He is known to have trudged some distance into a valley to see what kind of flowers were in a window box. The painting *Aspinwall* (Plate 9) combines two entirely different views of its subject: the background was sketched from the summit of a hill, and the foreground was studied at close range from the banks of the Allegheny River.[12] Not only is there no one spot from which the foreground and background can be seen simultaneously, but the two views actually point in different geographical directions, and the sites are not contiguous. Whereas academic landscape painting presents its subject from a single perspective and blurs or omits things that fall out of range, Kane studied each scene from multiple angles and rendered every part with the same precision of detail.

John Kane's paintings of Pittsburgh may be considered the heart and soul of an oeuvre that also included other subjects. It is probable that his remaining landscapes—views of Pennsylvania towns such as Harrisburg and Philadelphia, and of Scottish Highlanders (Plate 10)—were done largely from photographs and memory.[13] An added element of fantasy replaces the meticulous firsthand observation and interpretation that characterize the artist's depictions of his home turf. Without exception, his paintings embody cherished ideals and sentiments. He portrayed children with a wistful tenderness born of the separation from his own daughters and nurtured by his joyful old-age reunion with his grandchildren. An annual "Scotch Day" at Kennywood (Plate 13), a local amusement park, served as the inspiration for a number of paintings memorializing the artist's native land, for which he retained an abiding love. Equally devoted to the United States, Kane identified strongly with Lincoln, the poor boy who made good, and considered the Gettysburg Address "among the greatest works of great men." He executed at least two paintings of the Address, written out word for word against the background of an American flag (Plate 14).[14]

It is virtually impossible to date Kane's work before 1928, and the majority of the approximately 156 recorded oils[15] were probably executed after his public debut in 1927. Thus any attempt to posit a chronological development must be extremely tentative. To further confuse matters, Kane himself was inconsistent about titles, and after his death his paintings seem to have changed names almost every time they changed hands. Additional problems of identification were caused by his compulsive "touching up." Even after works had been exhibited and, in some cases, photographed, he continued to make modifications. It is entirely possible that many so-called "missing" paintings may actually have disappeared under a coat of the artist's own paint.

"Touching up" was a routine so meaningful to Kane that he immortalized it in two canvases (Plate 15). He habitually reworked his paintings intermittently over the course of a year or more, changing and adding and taking away until he

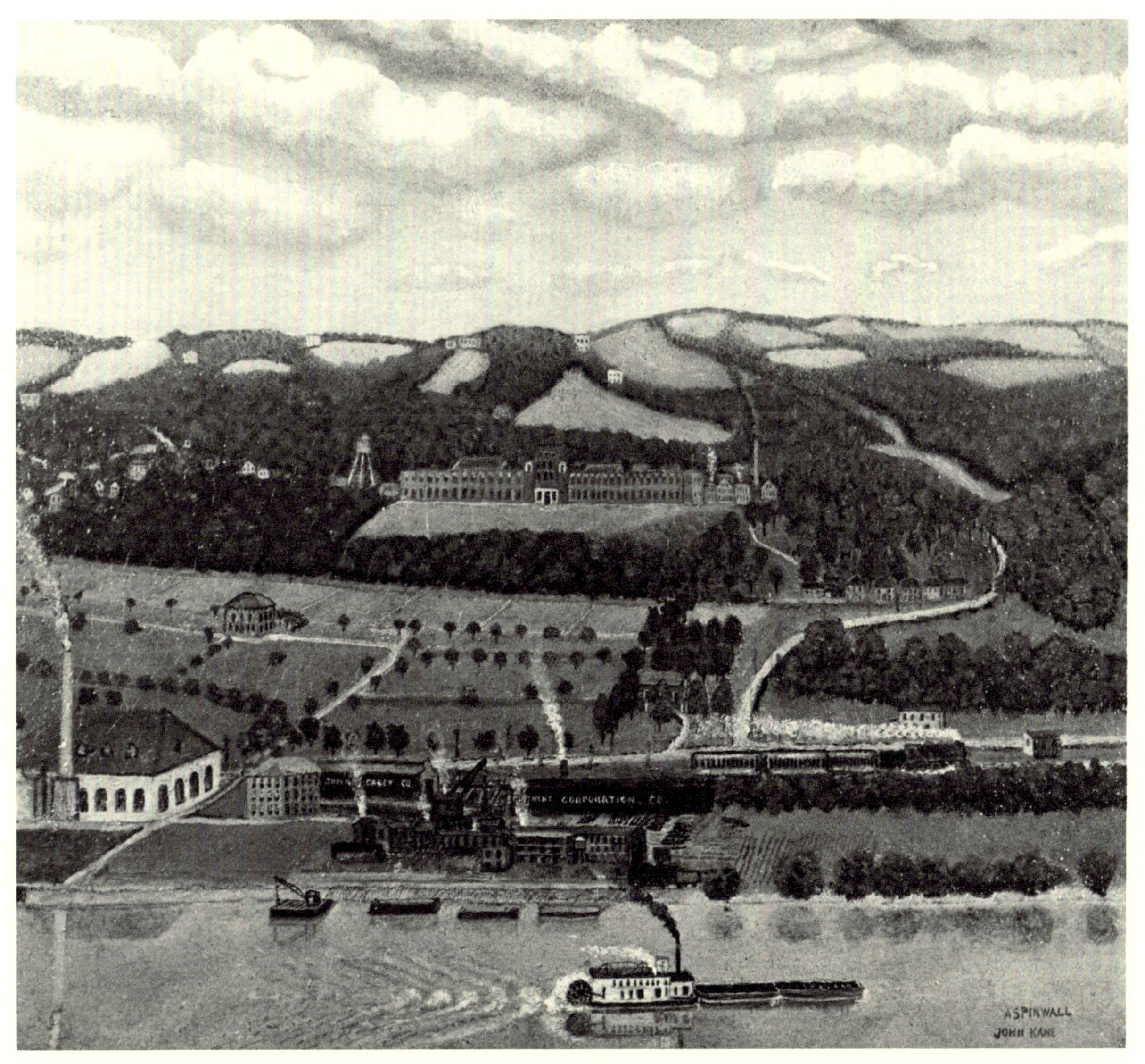

9. **Aspinwall**. Circa 1929-30. Board. 19″ x 21″. Canajoharie Library and Art Gallery.

was satisfied. As the unfinished *Juniata River* shows, he began with a light layer of simple, flat color. Forms, at this preliminary stage, were almost abstract. However, in the process of "touching up" the artist refined detail and enriched the composition by applying multiple coats of paint. The natural translucency of the oil pigment allowed the base coat to shine through subsequent layers, giving his colors unusual luminosity and depth.

Like all great folk painters, John Kane evolved his own techniques to substitute for those he would have learned in an art school. Similarly, he developed his own special method of landscape composition. This combination of technical and formal invention was the source of his original folk style: an ad hoc approach none the worse for its failure to adhere to academic conventions, and possibly richer for its intimate relationship to the artist's expressive goals. In the final analysis, Kandinsky was not wrong in his contention that the folk artist is more purely guided by his creative instincts, more original in his ultimate solutions, than is the academician.

John Kane's particular vision is unique in our time. If, as has been suggested, he is the foremost painter of the industrial scene, it is an honor for which there has been little competition. We may learn as schoolchildren that industry and technology made America great, but as adults we succumb to the prevalent cynicism regarding this nation's path to glory. Pittsburgh is inevitably associated with some of the less attractive moments in our history: it is the one-time home of billowing smokestacks, exploitative robber barons, and violent strikes. Kane's bucolic hillsides come as a surprise to those who are unfamiliar with the city's unusual combination of rural and urban characteristics. The artist painted slums without squalor, industry without horror—omissions that, to more socially minded critics, seem politically naive and, to others, are merely inexplicable.

How could an artist celebrate something whose ugliness is universally acknowledged? Why didn't Kane see what we see? Or, more to the point, what did he see that we do not? For when John Kane looked at the billowing smokestacks of a bustling factory, he saw the majestic surge of prosperity. When he looked at the warm brown brick walls of a tenement, he saw a myriad gentle, noble lives, rounded out with simple ambitions and the reliable trot of the milkman's horse. Walking along the many bridges that link Pittsburgh's hills and cross its railroad tracks and roadways, Kane gazed into the lush valleys and found, in the little houses and trees and trains and cars, the living embodiment of the American dream that the rest of us have long ago given up for lost.

Note

All quotations, unless otherwise attributed, have been taken from Marie McSwigan's *Sky Hooks*, as reprinted in Leon Anthony Arkus's catalogue raisonné, *John Kane, Painter* (Pittsburgh: University of Pittsburgh Press, 1971).

The paintings reproduced in the catalogue are executed in oil on canvas unless otherwise indicated. A separate checklist describing in detail all 68 exhibited works is available on request.

Footnotes

1. An article in the *Pittsburgh Sun Telegraph*, published on August 12, 1934, suggests that Dasburg actually forced the decision by threatening to veto all the other entries unless the jury voted for Kane's.

2. *The Detroit News*, December 12, 1930. In February 1931, possibly at the insistence of Mrs. Kane, the couple moved to a larger apartment on Ophelia Street, where they stayed until that summer, when they moved to their final address at 1700 Fifth Avenue.

3. Kane's compassion for his fellow artists, in view of their spiteful jealousy of him, is particularly touching. Penelope Redd, art critic for the *Pittsburgh Sun Telegraph*, recalled that the painfully shy man would often bring colleagues to her office and ask her to help them.

4. *The Art Digest*, November 1, 1929.

5. One of the reasons Kane remained relatively impoverished was that there was no real folk art market during his lifetime. Depression-era economics did not help matters, nor did the fact that Kane's independent nature caused him to reject the offers of dealers who would have promoted him in exchange for exclusive rights to his artistic production. Instead, Kane set his own prices according to the scale that he, as a poor laborer, had been accustomed to. He easily fell prey to unscrupulous collectors, one of whom, according to his daughter, Margaret Corbett, took advantage of the artist's inability to handle liquor and apparently absconded with a number of major works.

6. Around 1910, a bank clerk in Akron mistakenly wrote the name "K-A-N-E," and the artist obligingly adopted the new spelling.

7. Although Kane refers several times to his use of pastel, no such works have ever turned up.

8. According to Margaret Corbett. Valentine Dudensing, the first representative of the Kane estate, undoubtedly wanted to ensure that scandals of the kind that had plagued the artist during his lifetime did not recur.

9. To date, 71 sheets of sketches have been catalogued, many containing drawings on both sides. Of these, 35 are figural studies and 85 are landscapes.

10. *The Bulletin Index, Pittsburgh's Weekly Newsmagazine*, February 16, 1933.

11. A careful attempt to retrace Kane's steps shows that he usually relied on the natural vantage points offered by bridges and cemeteries, which are often located on hills and offer unobstructed panoramas. In picking an initial site, he did not stray far from the paved roads or pathways, though he might go out of his way to obtain supplemental information. In his autobiography, he tells of climbing a smokestack to take pictorial notes on a vista he admired.

12. To further confuse matters, the area depicted, though titled "Aspinwall" by the artist, is actually located in O'Hara Township, just east of Aspinwall.

13. There are no known pencil sketches for these paintings, which suggests that the artist did not have the opportunity to study the scenes in person.

14. A second version of this painting (Plate 14), thought to have been lost, was recently discovered on the back of the painting *George Washington* (Arkus 80). Although this painting does not exactly fit the artist's description of the lost work, Marie McSwigan, in her introduction to *Sky Hooks*, describes a two-sided painting of Washington and Lincoln that underwent much "touching up" during the last year of Kane's life. Leon Arkus suggests that the missing picture looked like the version depicted in *Touching Up* (Plate 15 and Arkus 4), but it could be that the painting was "touched up" beyond all recognition.

15. Since the publication of Leon Arkus's catalogue raisonné, a handful of additional works have come to light, and the Kane estate's records have slightly swollen the number of documented but unaccounted for paintings.

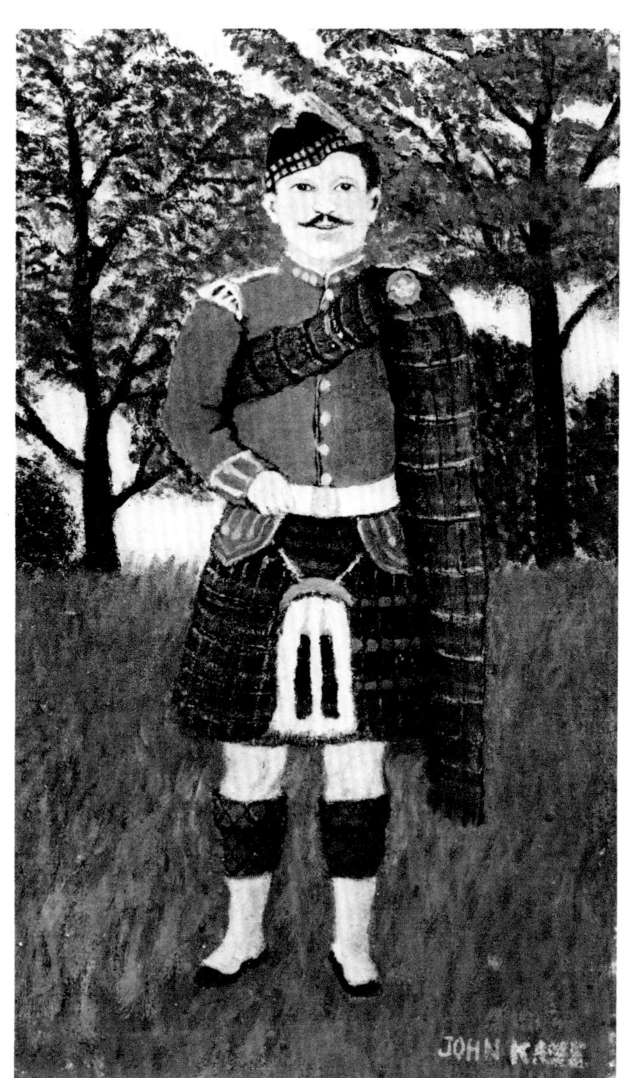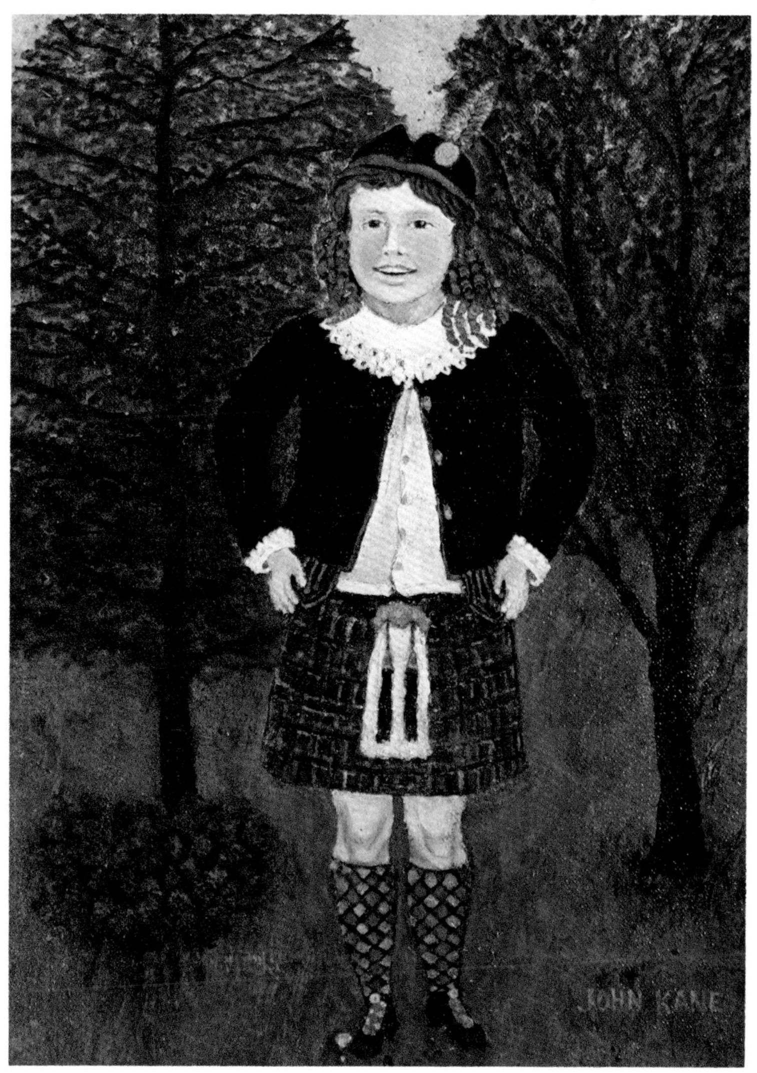

10. **Highlander**. Board. 13¾″ x 8″.
11. **Lassie in Kilts**. 15⅛″ x 11½″. Hirshhorn Museum and Sculpture Garden, Smithsonian Institution.

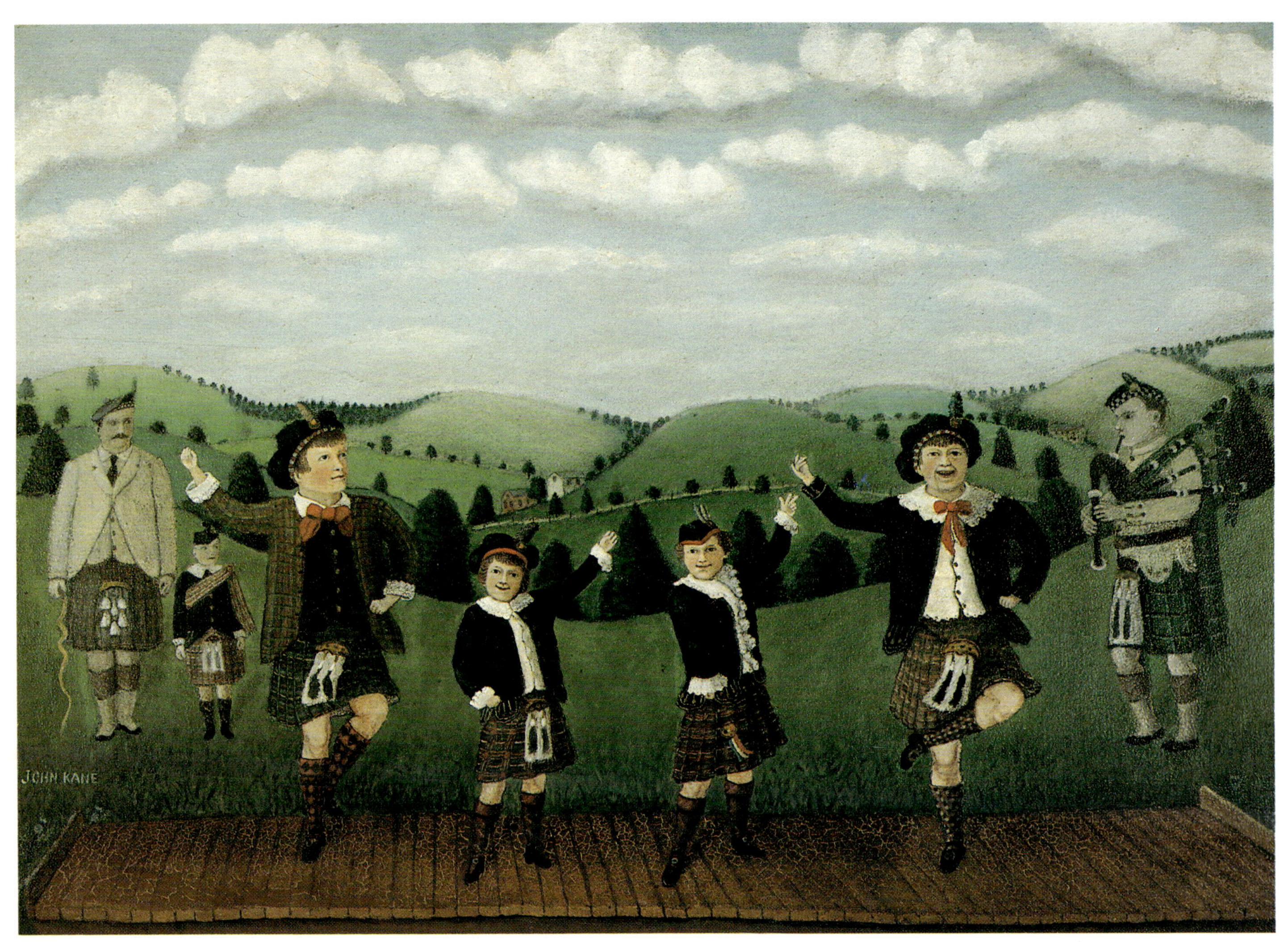

12. **Highland Hollow**. 26½″ x 36½″. Museum of Art, Carnegie Institute;
Gift of Mary and Leland Hazard, 1961.

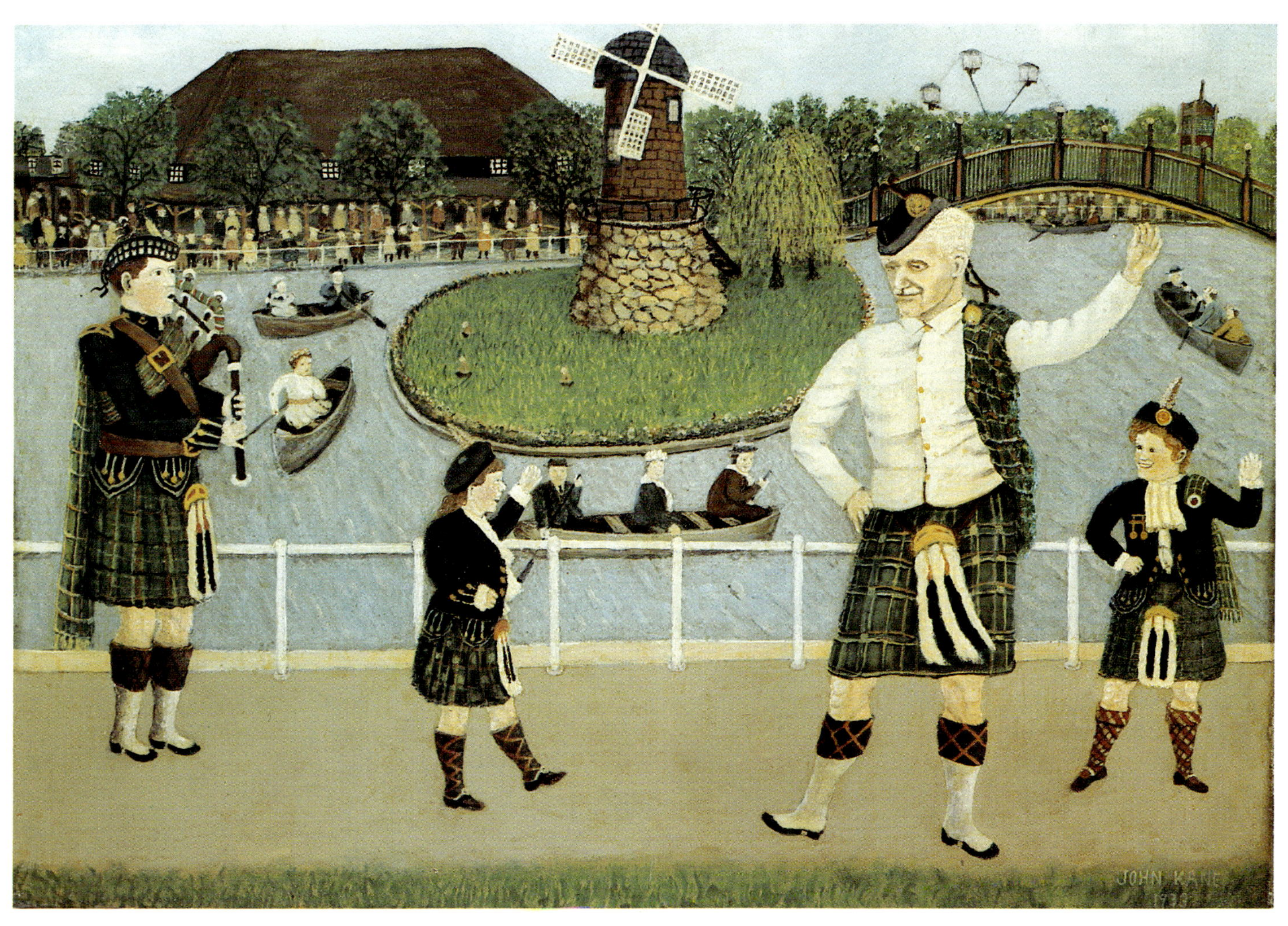

13. **Scotch Day at Kennywood.** 1933. 19⅞″ x 27⅛″. The Museum of Modern Art;
Gift of Mr. and Mrs. Albert Lewin, 1953.

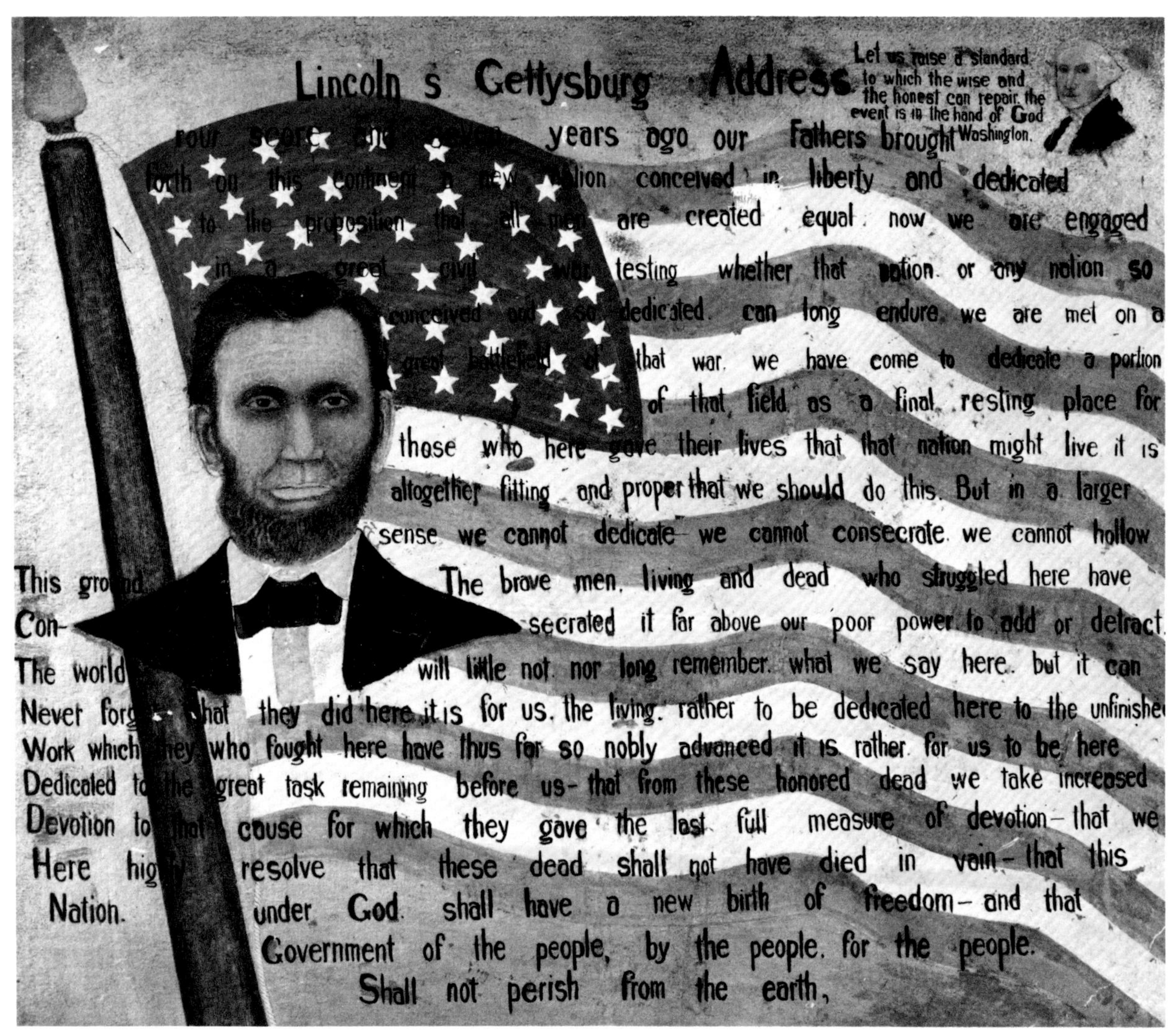

14. Lincoln's Gettysburg Address (Large Version). 28″ x 32″.

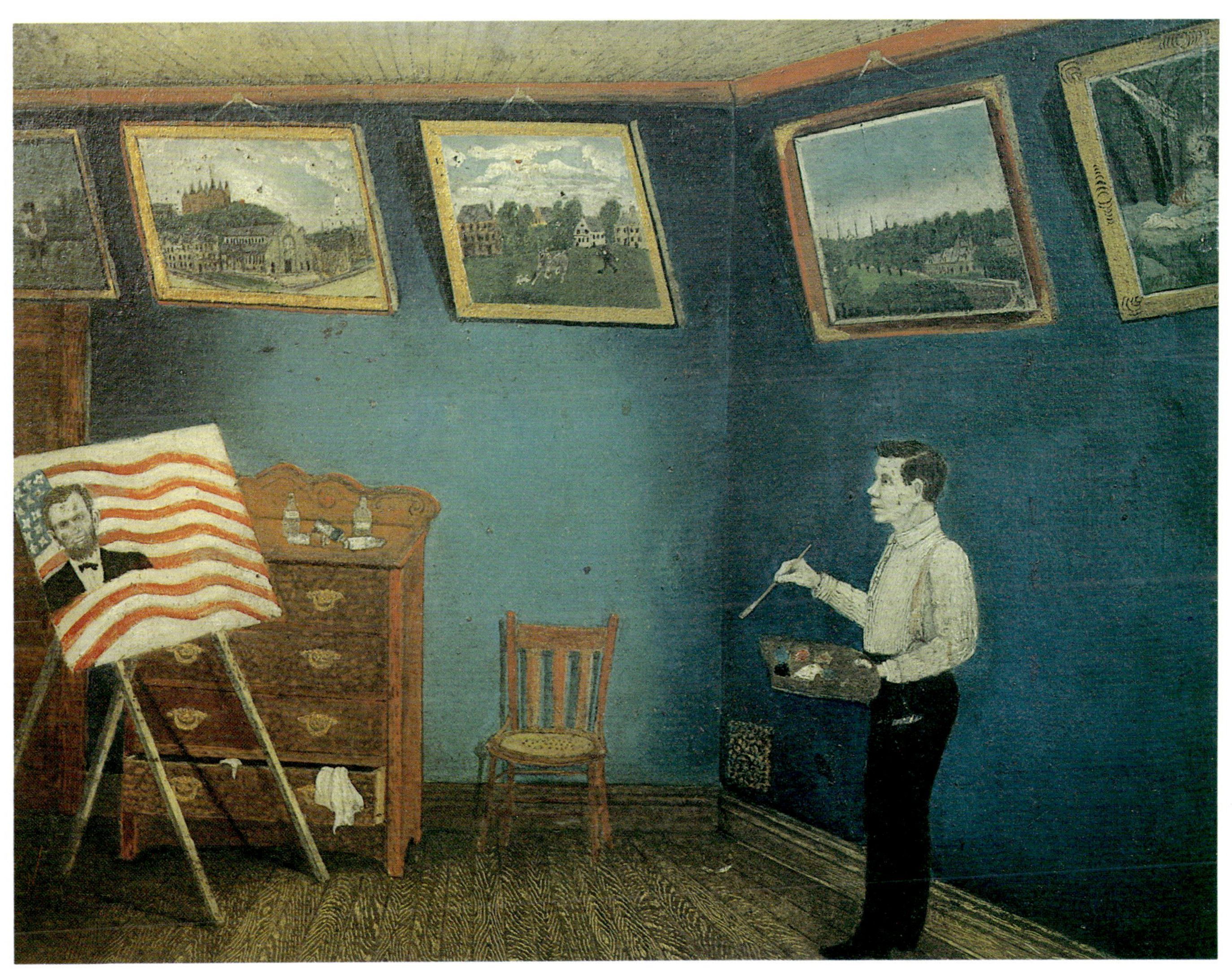

15. **Touching Up (Small Version).** Circa 1927. Board. 15¼″ x 19¼″.

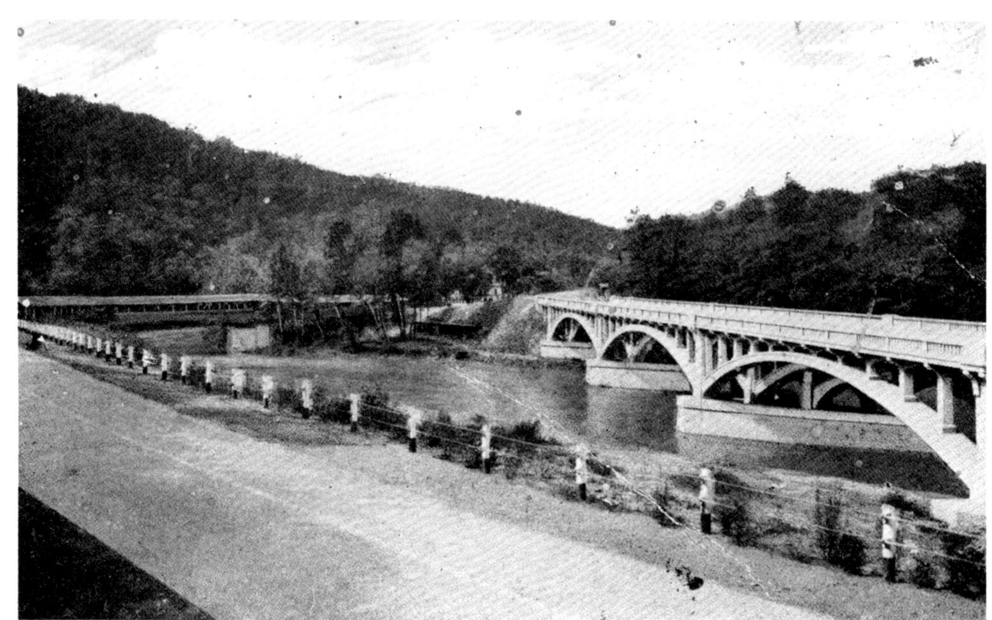

16. **Riverside View.** Anonymous photograph. Courtesy Leon Anthony Arkus.

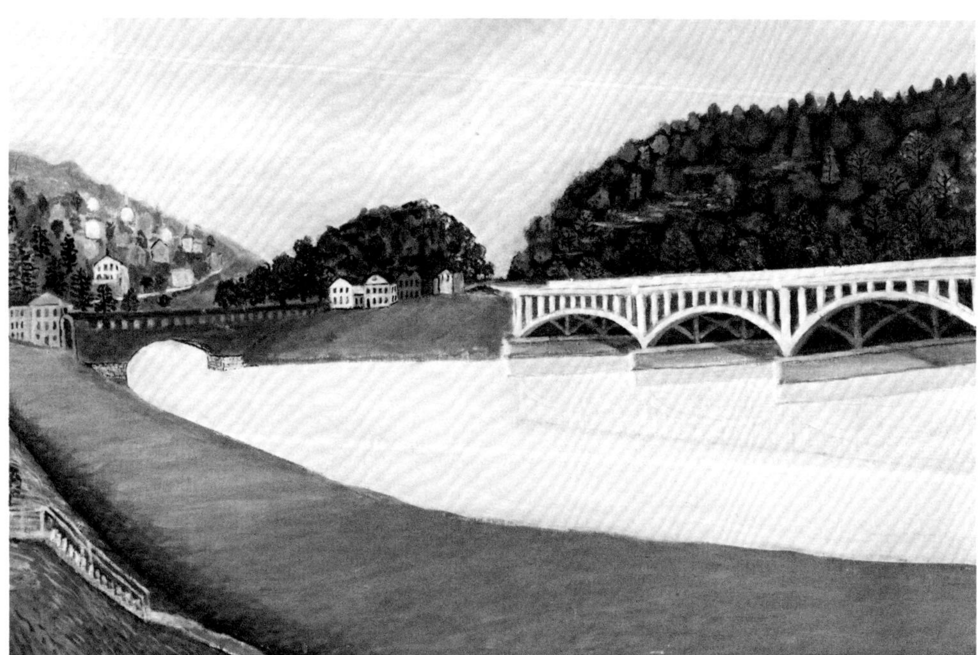

17. **Juniata River (Unfinished).** 28" x 42".

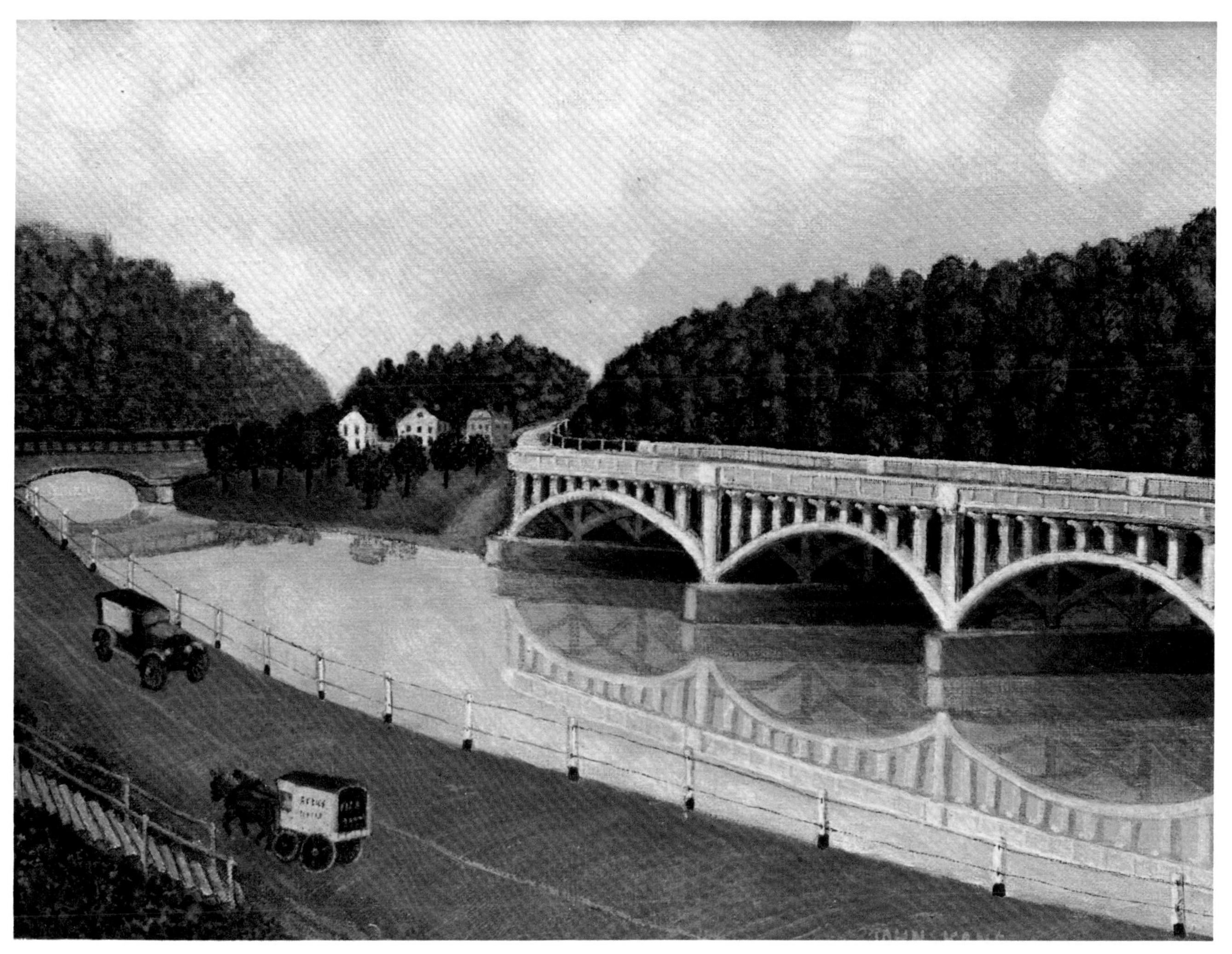

18. **Juniata River**. 1932. 15¾″ x 20. Albright-Knox Art Gallery; The Room of Contemporary Art Fund, 1939.

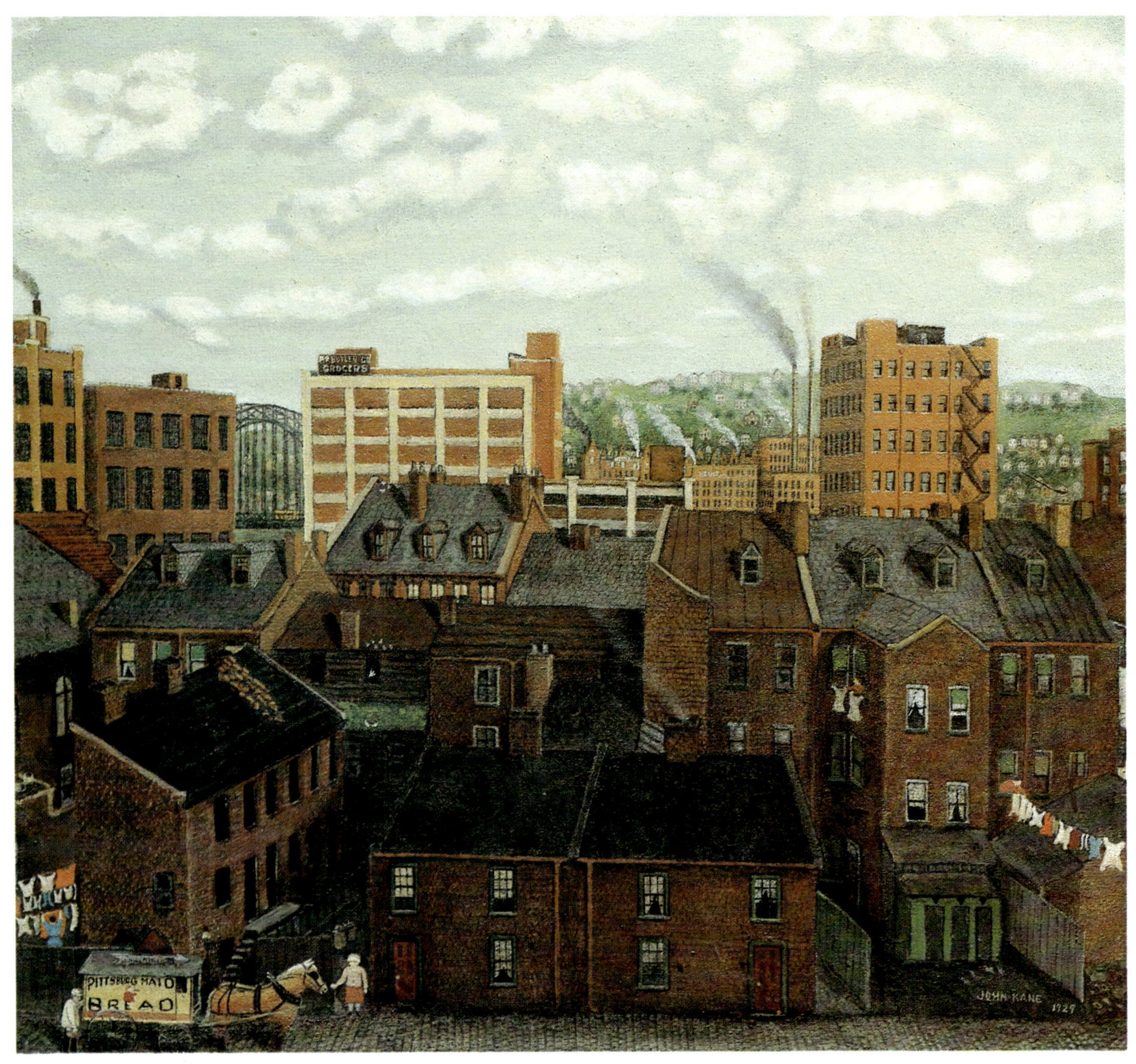

19. **Across the Strip.** 1929. 32¼″ x 34¼″. The Phillips Collection.

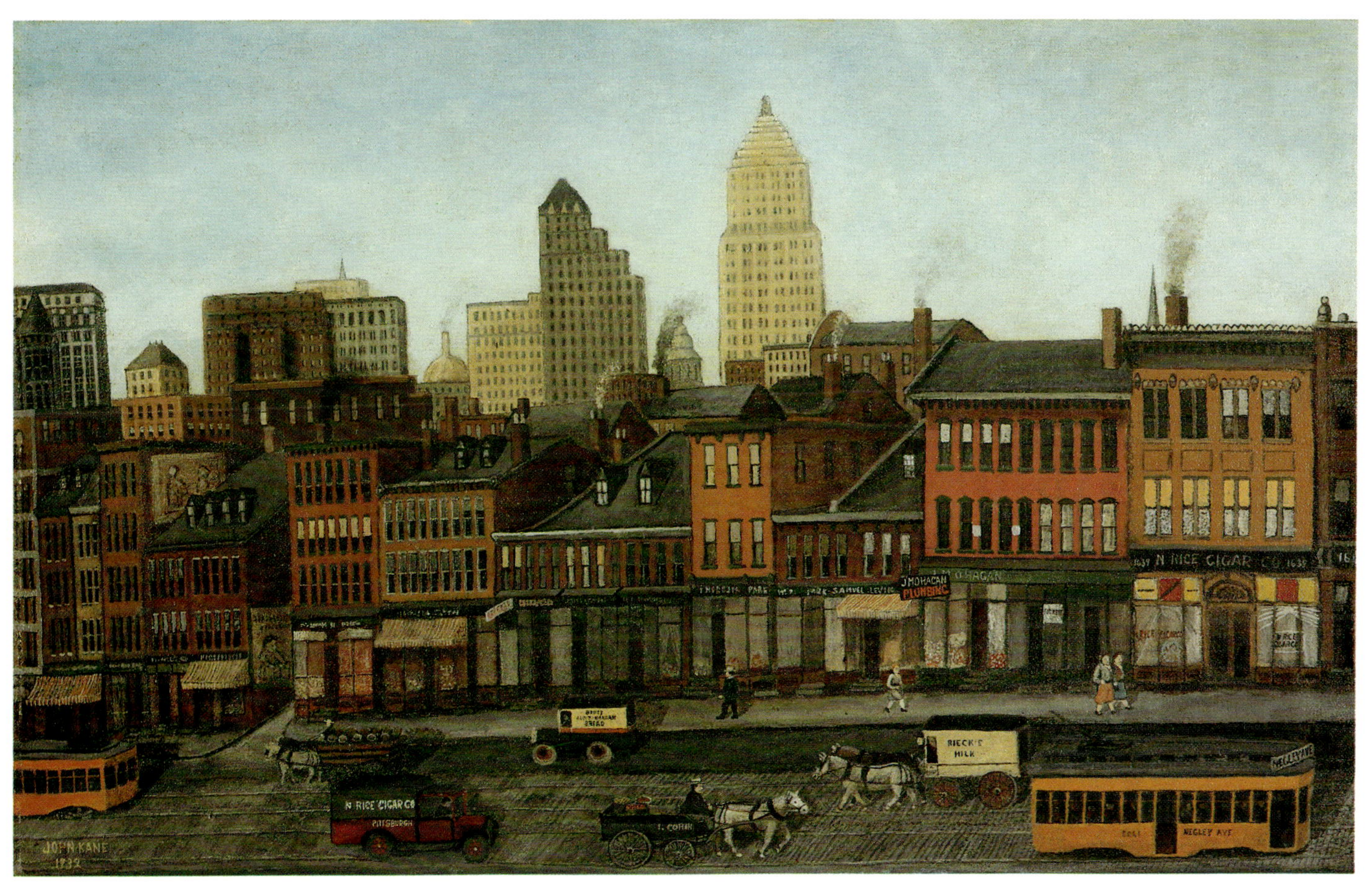

20. **From My Studio Window**. 1932. 22⅜″ x 34⅜″. The Metropolitan Museum of Art;
Bequest of Miss Adelaide Milton de Groot (1876-1967), 1967.

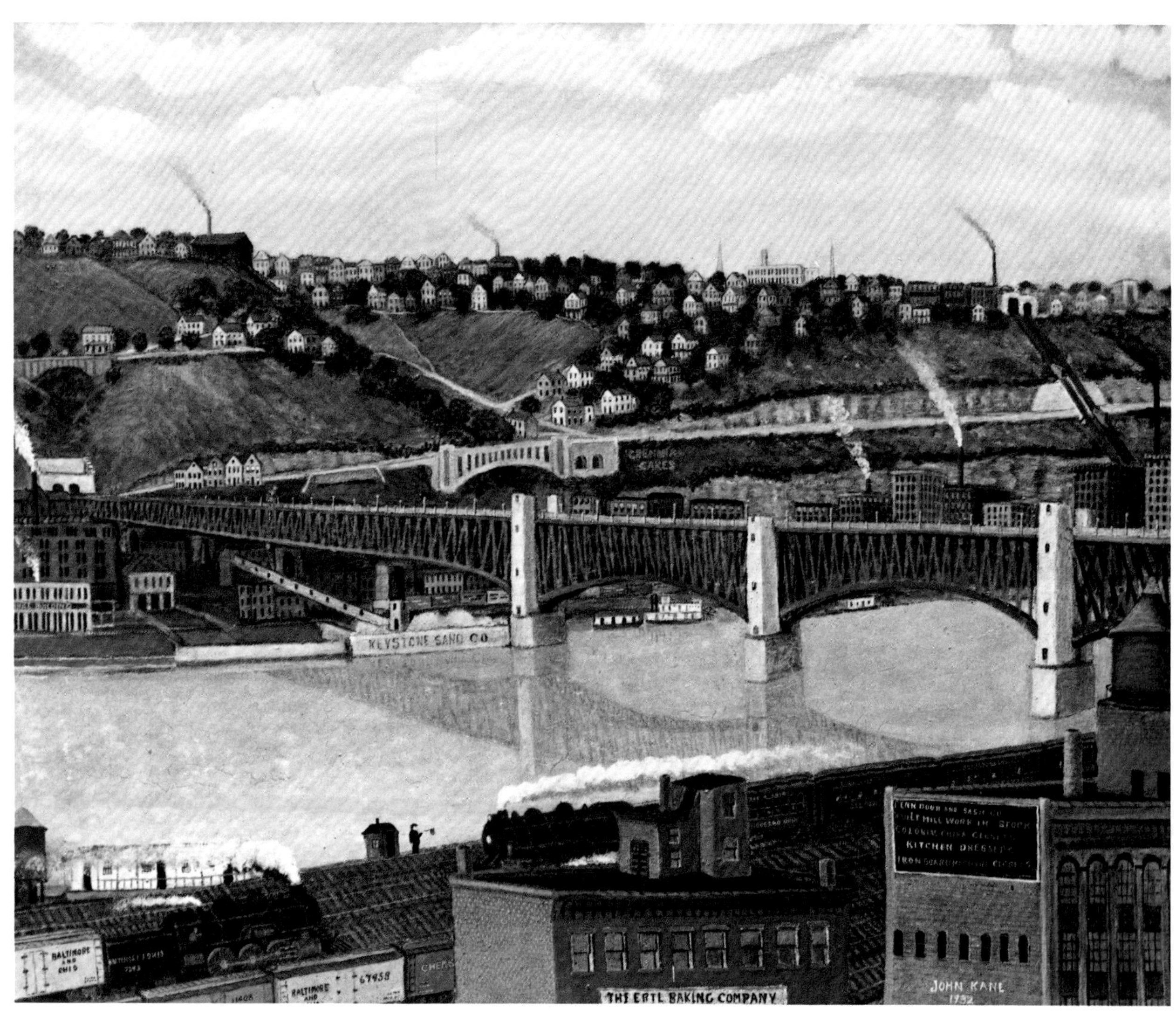

21. **Liberty Bridge**. 1932. 28″ x 33″. Addison Gallery of American Art, Phillips Academy.

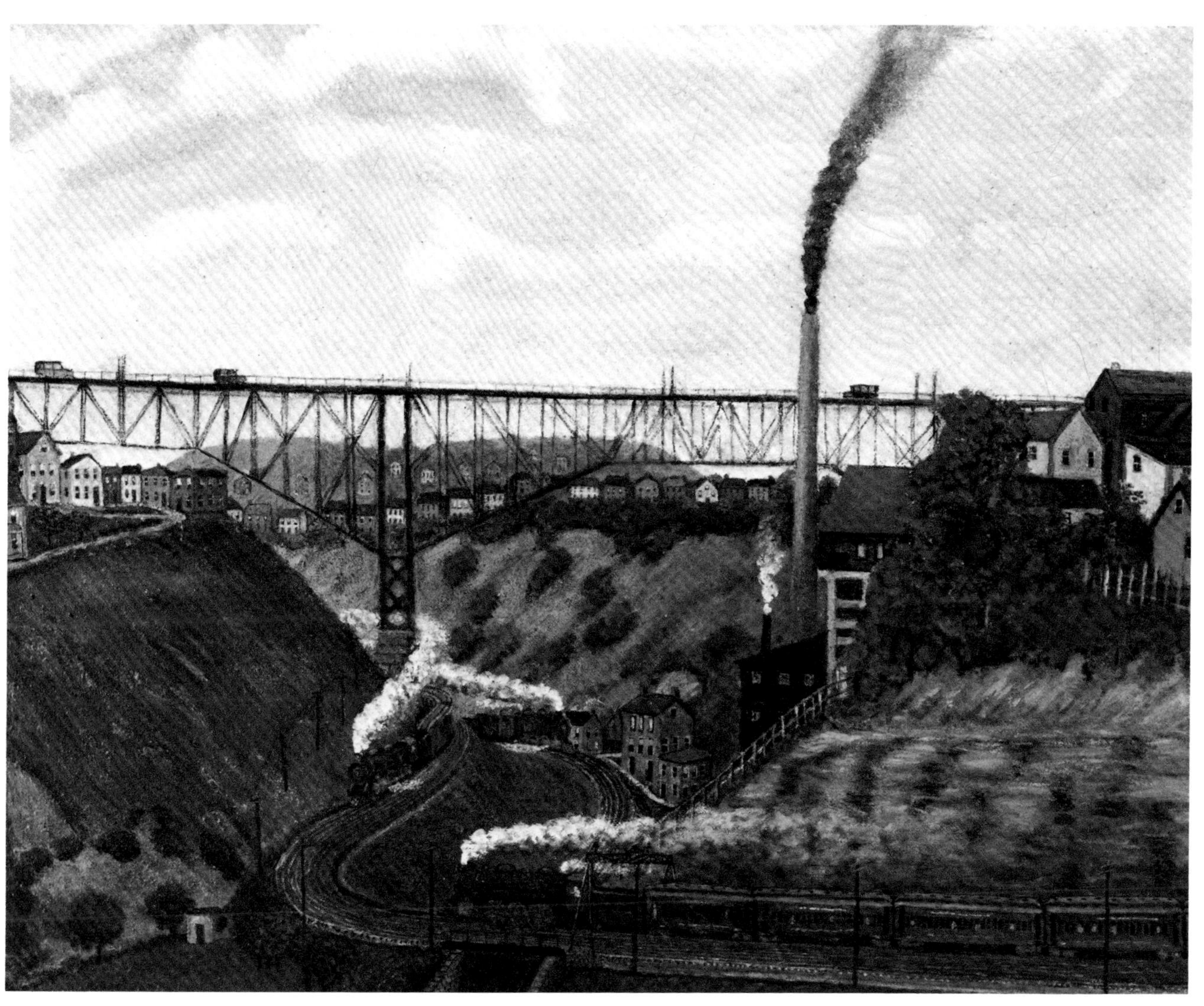

22. **Bloomfield Bridge**. Circa 1930. 20″ x 24″. Museum of Art, Carnegie Institute;
Gift of Mr. and Mrs. James H. Beal, 1981.

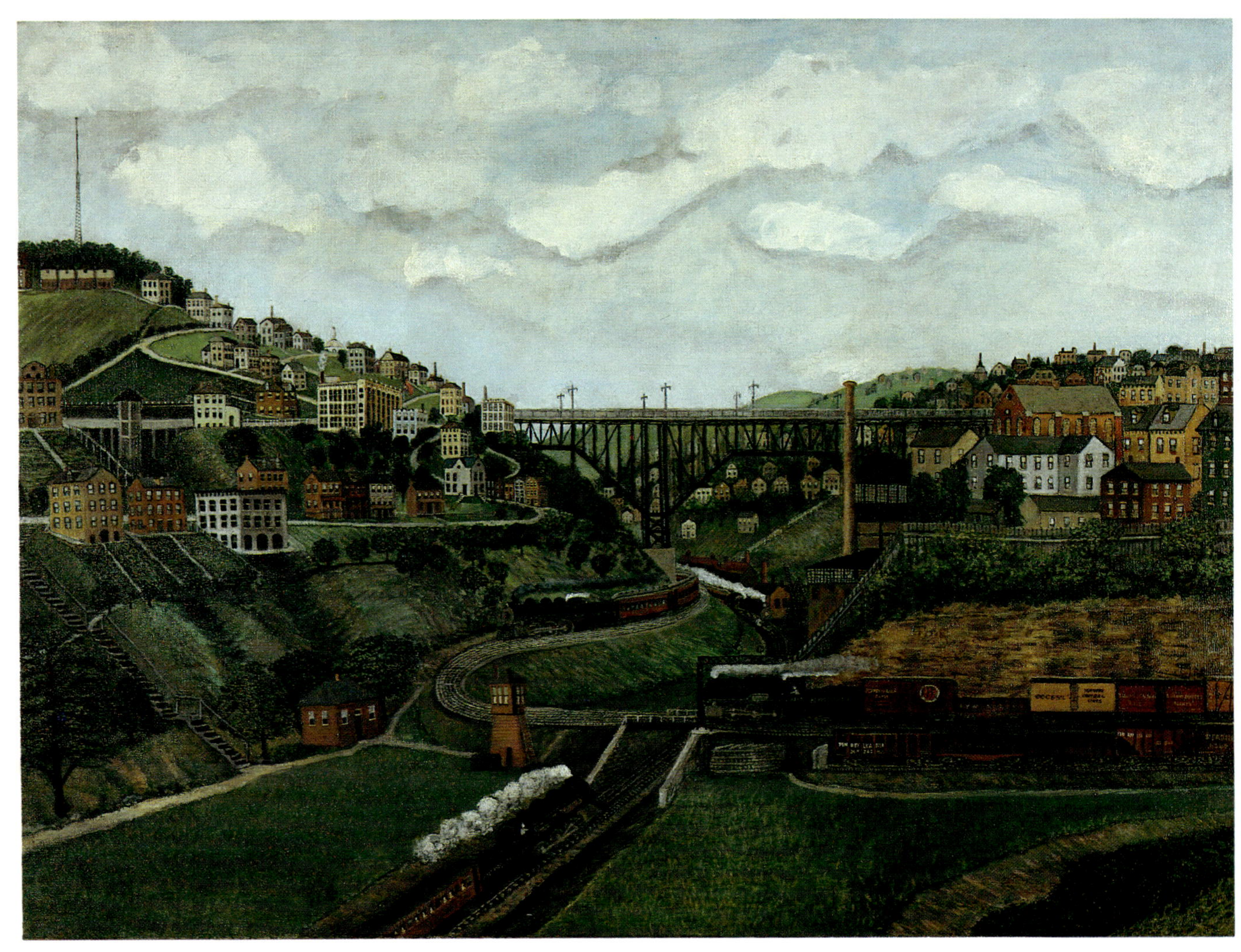

23. **Crossing the Junction.** 1933-34. 35½″ x 47½″. H.J. Heinz Company.

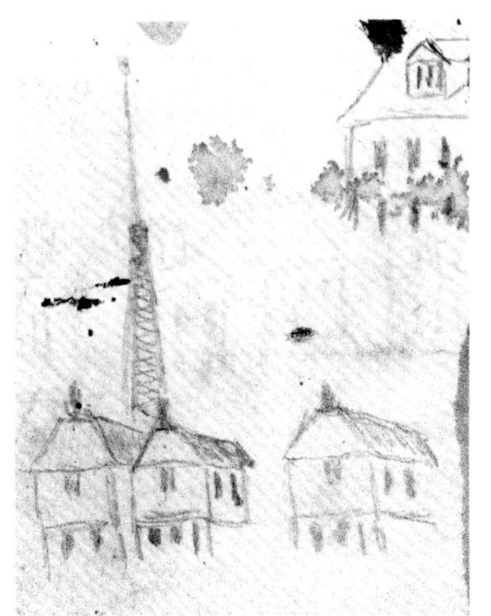

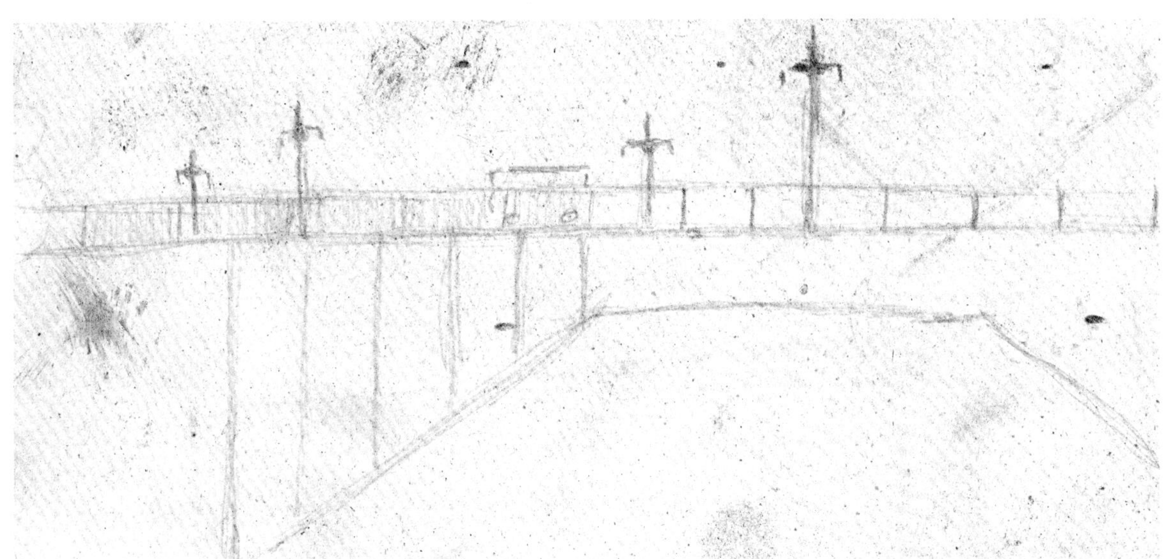

24. Study for **Crossing the Junction**. Circa 1933-34. Pencil on paper. 4⅞″ x 7⅞″.
25. Study for **Crossing the Junction**. Circa 1933-34. Pencil on paper. 9″ x 12¾″.
26. **Bloomfield Bridge**. Pencil on paper. 10¼″ x 11¾″.

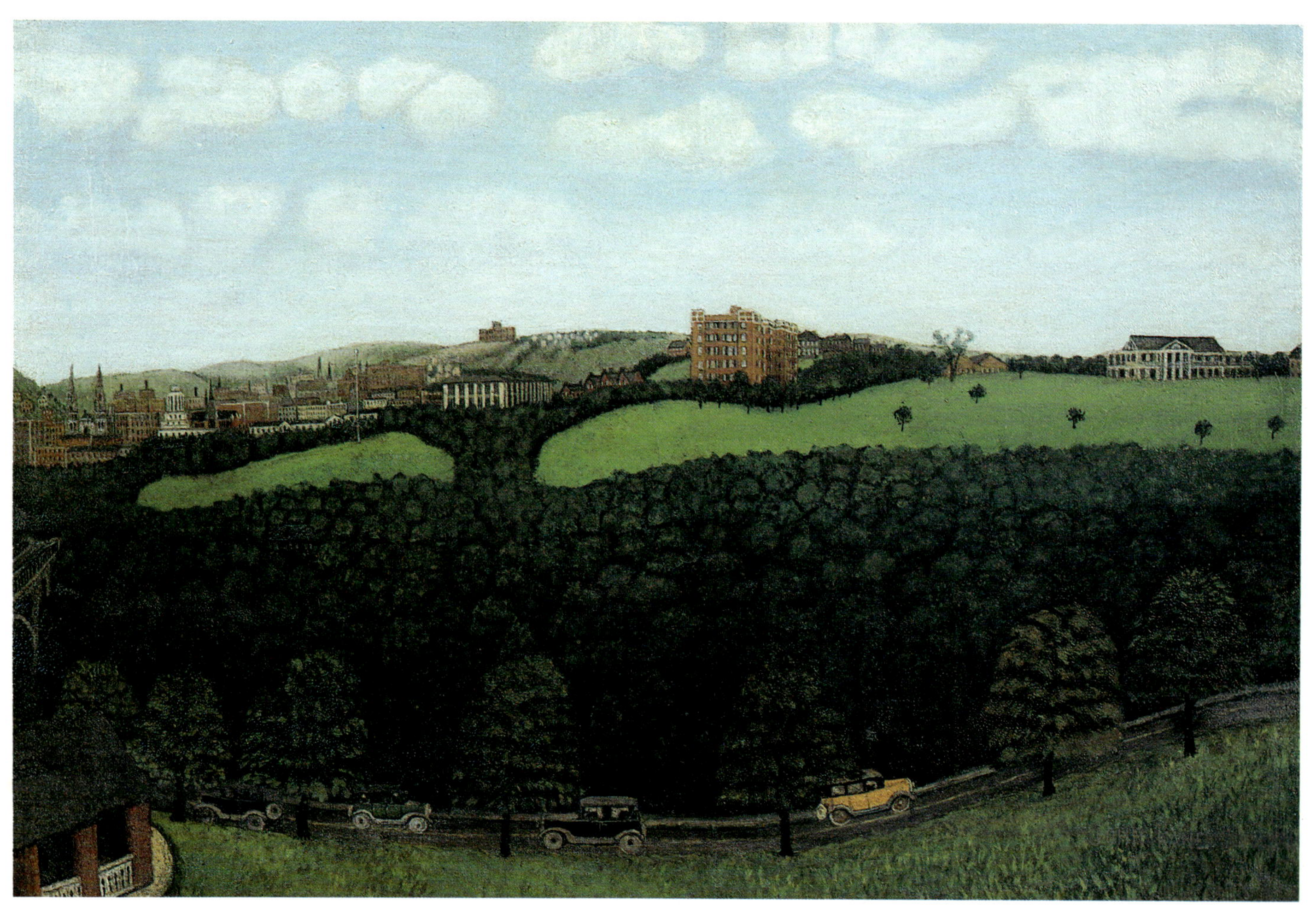

27. **Panther Hollow**. Circa 1930-31. 20″ x 29″. Whitney Museum of American Art; Purchase, 1935.

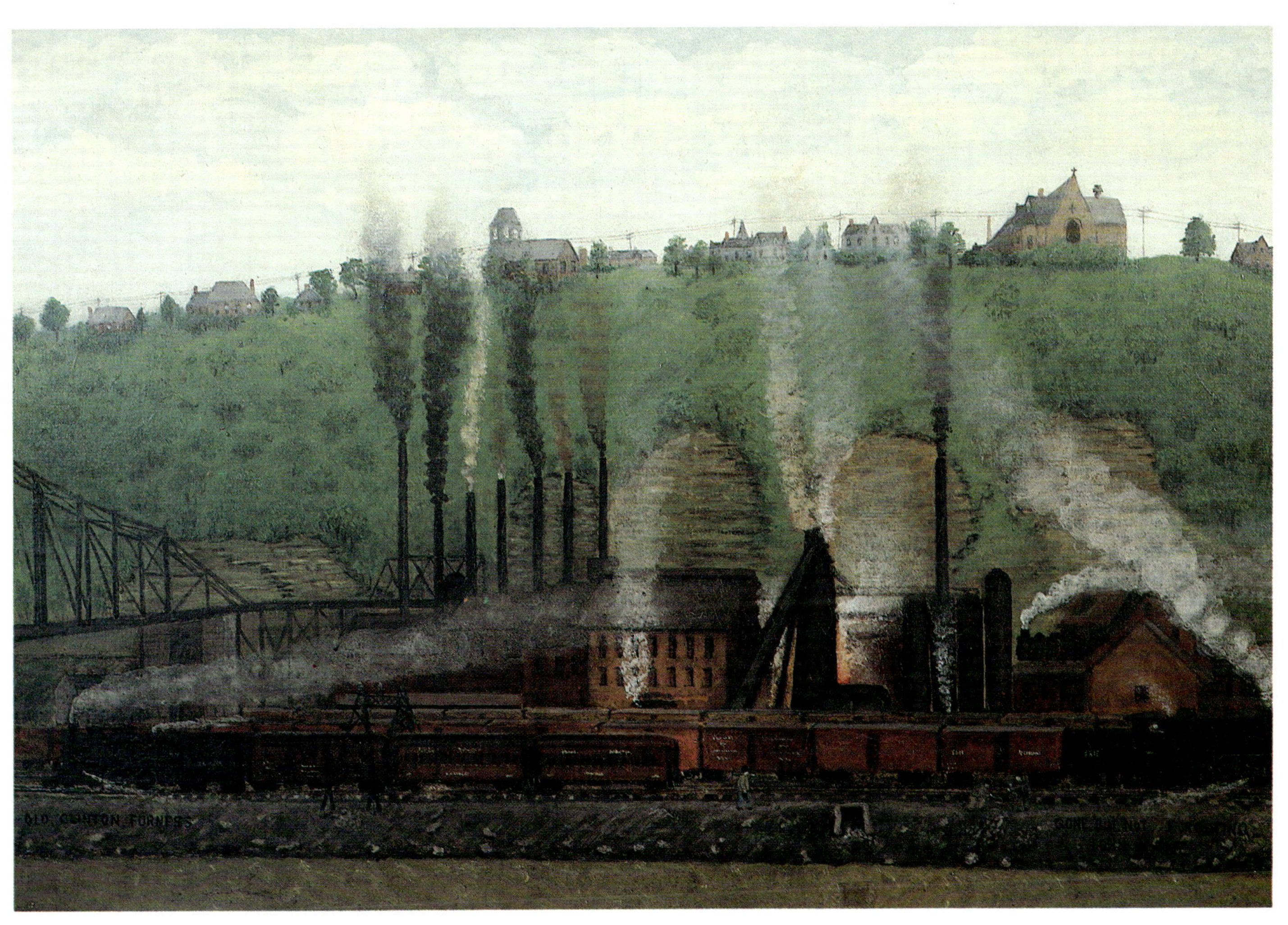

28. **Old Clinton Furnace**. Board. 18½″ x 22½″.

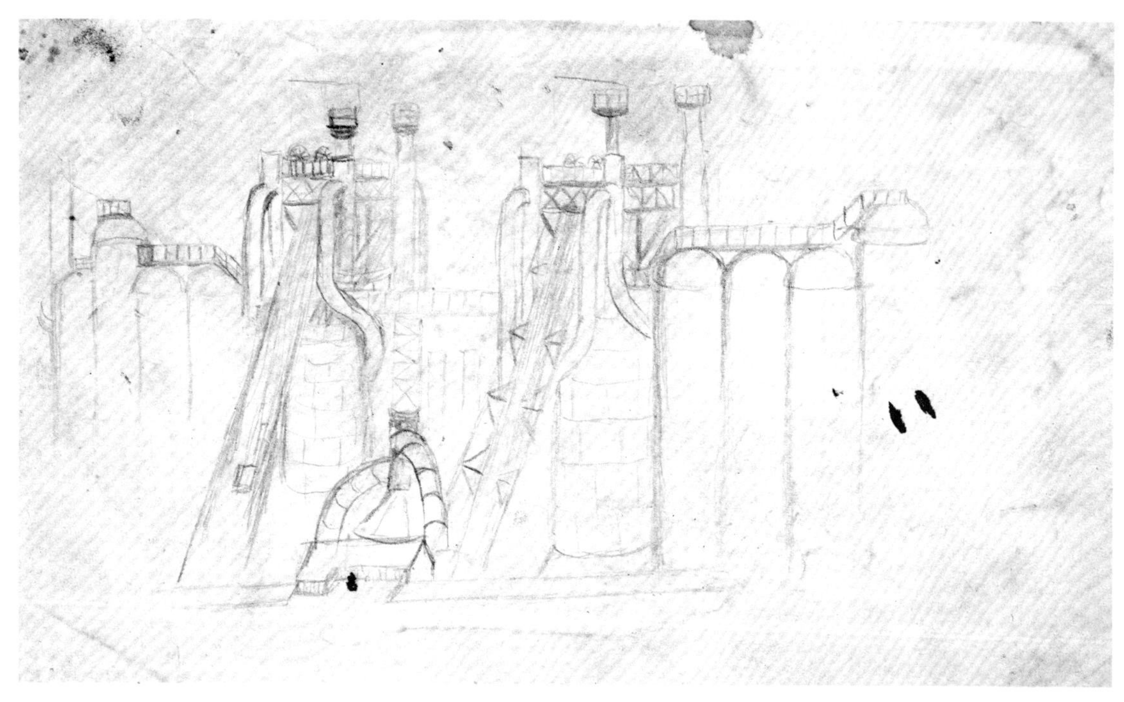

29. Study for **Monongahela Valley**. Circa 1931. Pencil on paper. 8⅜″ x 12¾″.

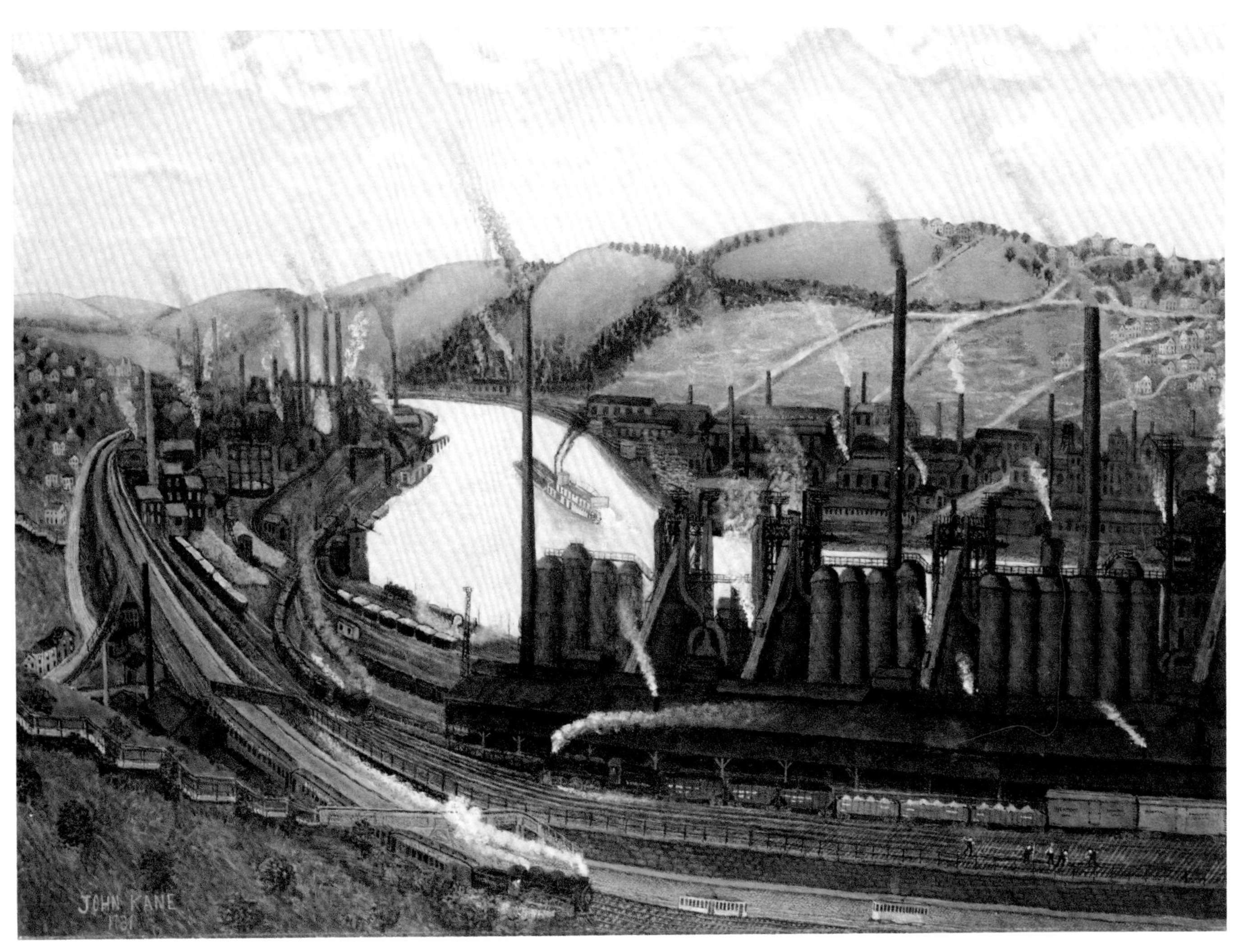

30. **Monongahela Valley**. 1931. 28″ x 35″. The Metropolitan Museum of Art; Bequest of Miss Adelaide Milton de Groot (1876-1967), 1967.

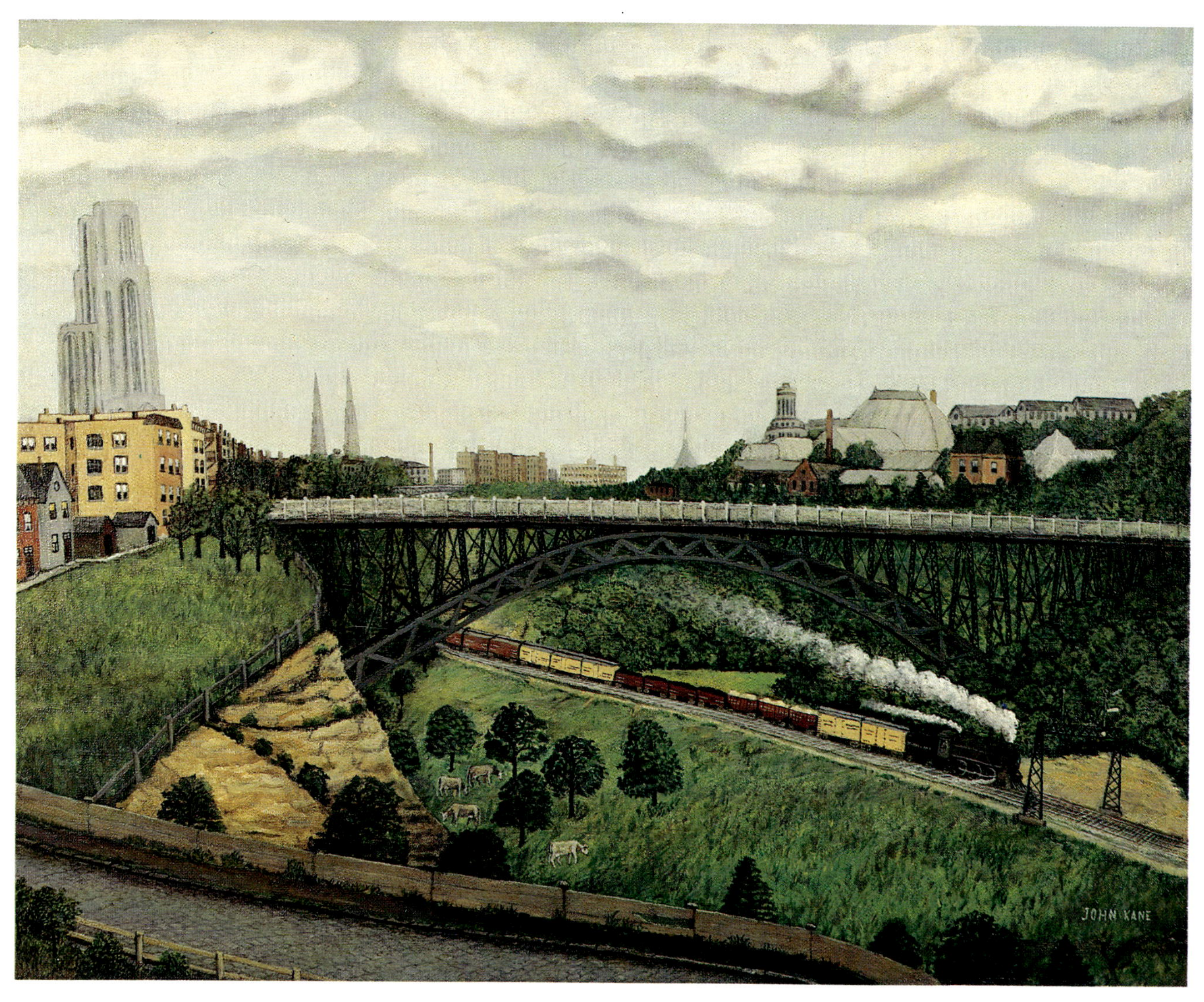

31. **Panther Hollow, Pittsburgh**. Circa 1933-34. 27¾" x 34". Museum of Art, Carnegie Institute; Gift of Mr. and Mrs. James F. Hillman, 1963.

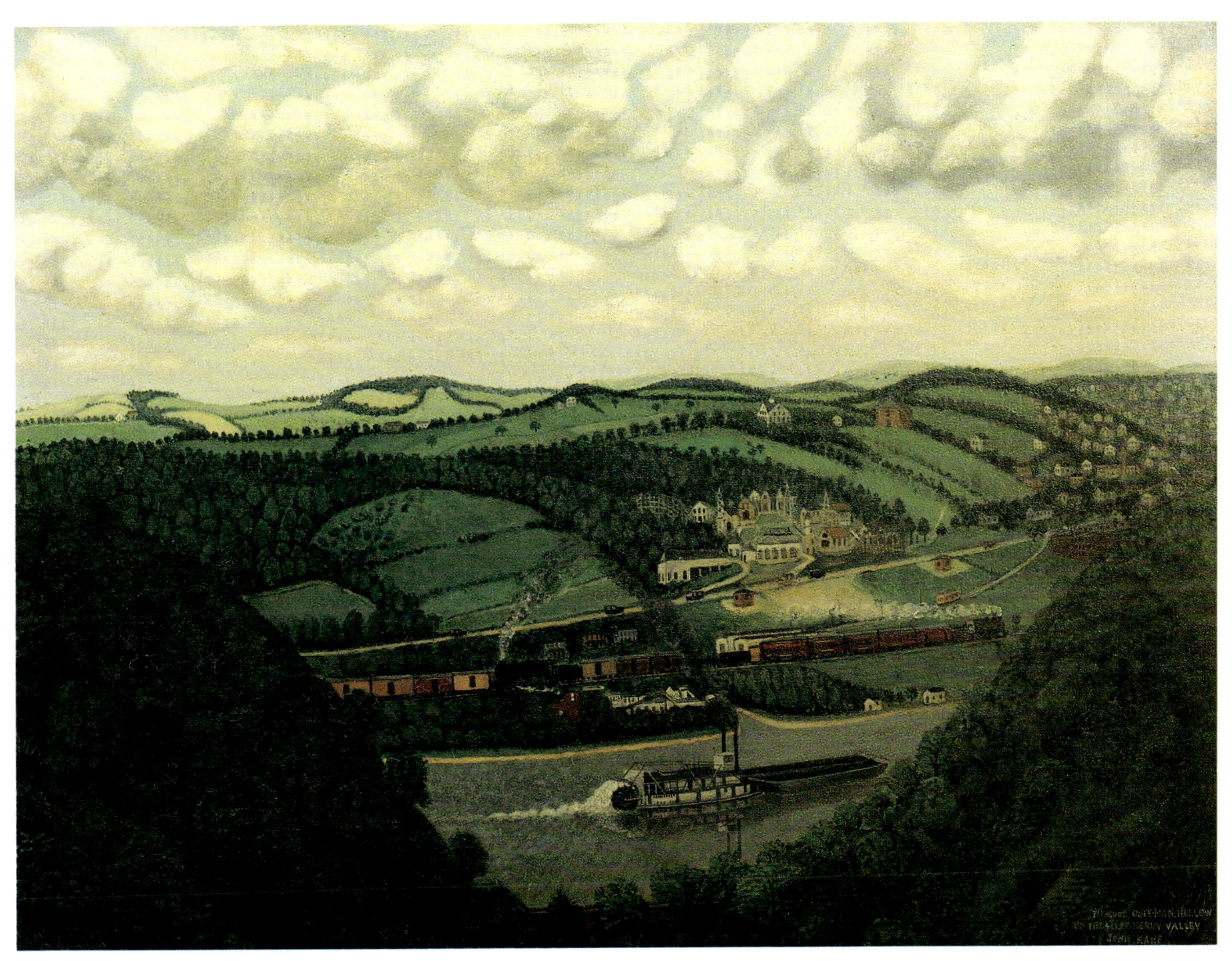

32. **Through Coleman Hollow, Up the Allegheny Valley.** Circa 1928. 30″ x 38⅝″. The Museum of Modern Art; Given Anonymously, 1941.

<u>Acknowledgements</u>

Not long ago, the Galerie St. Etienne took over representation of the estate of John Kane. While Kane is routinely included in museum surveys of folk art, the scarcity of his work has made one-man shows rare. The present effort, which includes many of his most important paintings, would not have been possible without the generous cooperation of our numerous lenders: Margaret Corbett, Mary Edwards, and the rest of the artist's family; the H.J. Heinz Company; the Addison Gallery of American Art, Phillips Academy, Andover, Massachusetts; the Albright-Knox Art Gallery, Buffalo, New York; the Canajoharie Library and Art Gallery, Canajoharie, New York; the Metropolitan Museum of Art, Museum of Modern Art, and Whitney Museum of American Art in New York; the Museum of Art, Carnegie Institute, Pittsburgh, Pennsylvania; the Hirshhorn Museum and Sculpture Garden, and the Phillips Collection in Washington, D.C.; and several private collectors who prefer to remain anonymous.

Last, but certainly not least, a very heartfelt word of thanks must go to the various people who helped us in researching our catalogue: to Margaret Corbett, the artist's daughter, whose collection of preliminary drawings provided the missing link in Kane's creative process; to Leon Anthony Arkus, who patiently answered all our many questions and gave us the benefit of his long-term involvement with the artist's work; and to John Lane and Henry Adams of the Museum of Art, Carnegie Institute, who put their entire archives at our disposal.

Hildegard Bachert
Jane Kallir
Directors, Galerie St. Etienne